color

Fluffy the Vulture

book 3

الكتاب الثالث

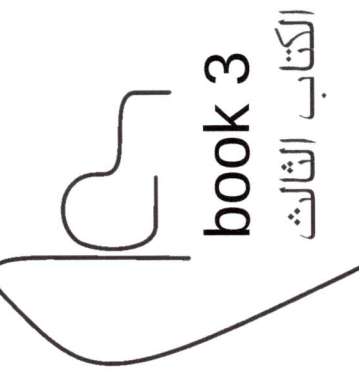

page numbers

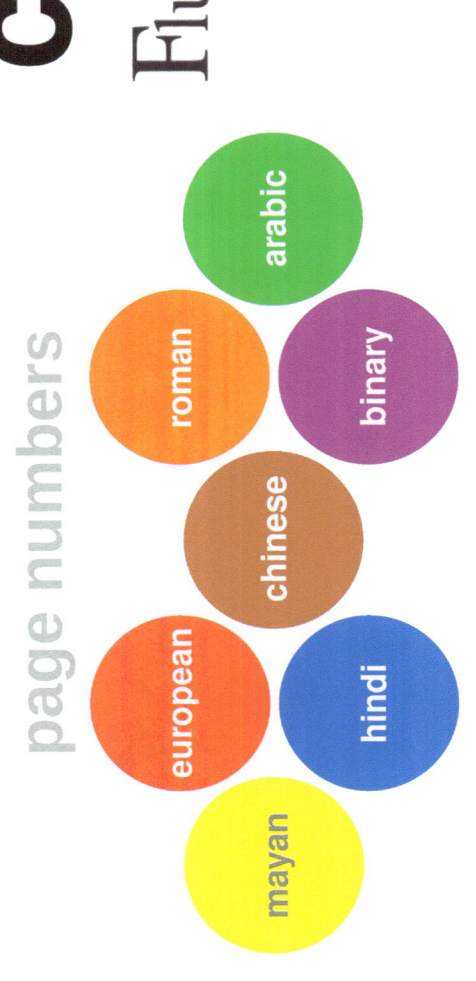

mayan · european · chinese · roman · arabic · hindi · binary

English
Chinese
Hungarian
French
Korean
Hawaiian
Spanish
Russian
Burmese

Japanese
Hindi
German
Italian
Norwegian
Portugese
Swahili
Greek
Bengali

Arabic
Thai
Polish
Dutch
Hebrew
Vietnamese
Tagalog
Czech
Farsi

color, Fluffy the Vulture, by William Zicker
copyright 2011, Belifan Publishing, www.belifan.com
book 3 in a series
www.FluffyTheVulture.com

dedicated to the Molvik family
Håvard, Amanda, Scarlett and Alexander

For since the beginning of the world men have not heard, nor perceived by the ear, neither hath the eye seen, O God, beside thee, what he hath prepared for him that waiteth for him.

Isaiah 64:4

But as it is written, Eye hath not seen, nor ear heard, neither have entered into the heart of man, the things which God hath prepared for them that love him.

Corinthians 2:9

Human perception and communication have limits.

Here we see 25 languages - most people can read only a few.

Look how much of the electromagnetic spectrum is invisible to the human eye!

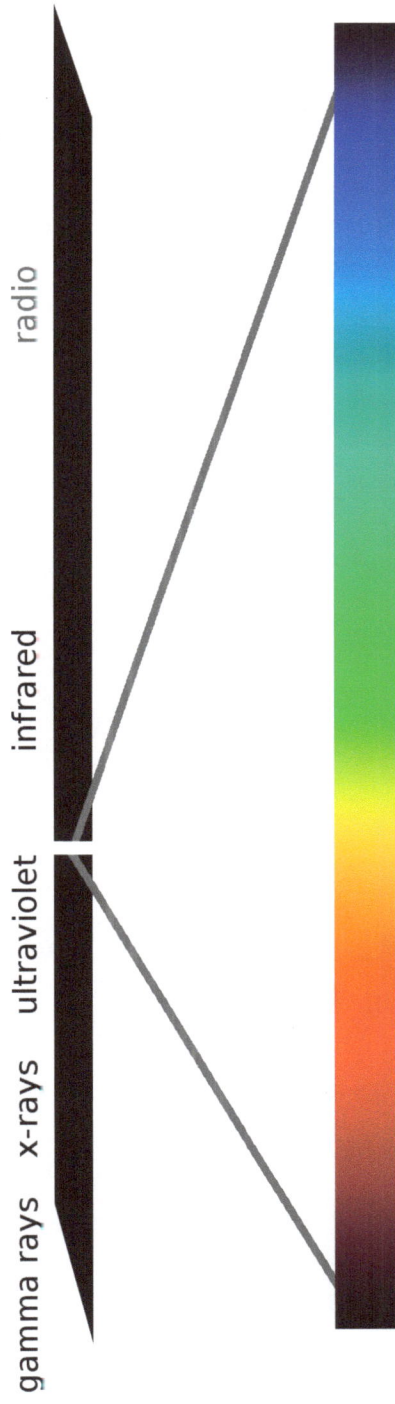

gamma rays   x-rays   ultraviolet   infrared   radio

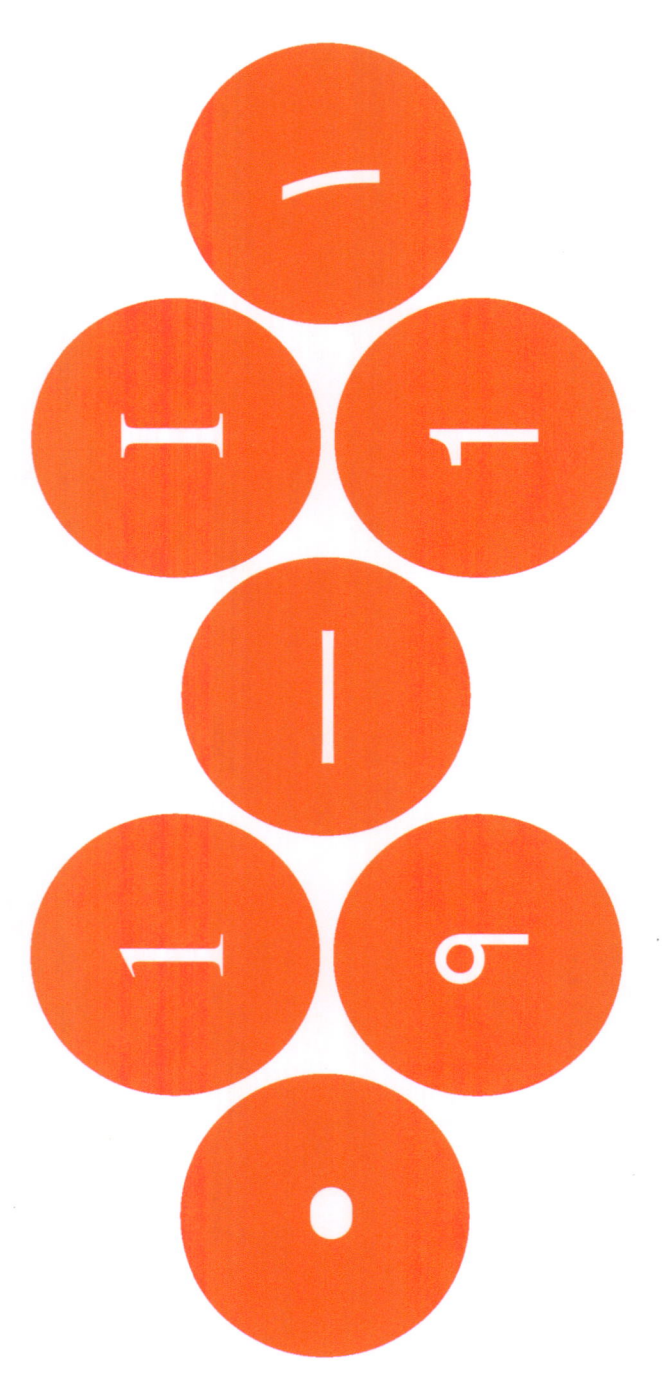

أحمر

אדום

قرمز

लाल
लाल

নীল

czerwony
rood

đỏ
pula
červená

赤
लाल
rot
rosso
rød
vermelho
nyekundu
κόκκινο
लाल

red
赤
piros
rouge
빨간색
ula ula
rojo
красный
ಕೆಂಪು

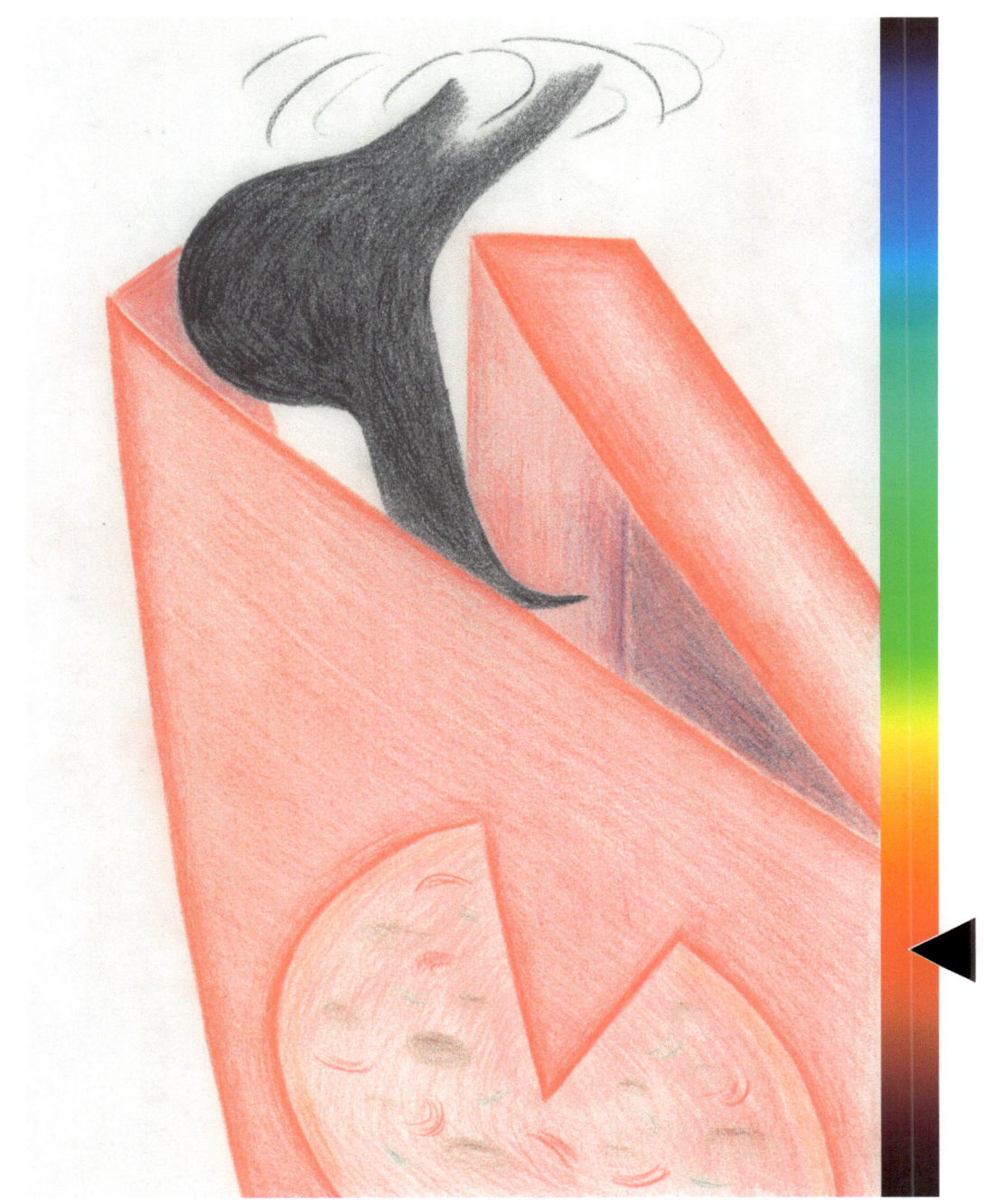

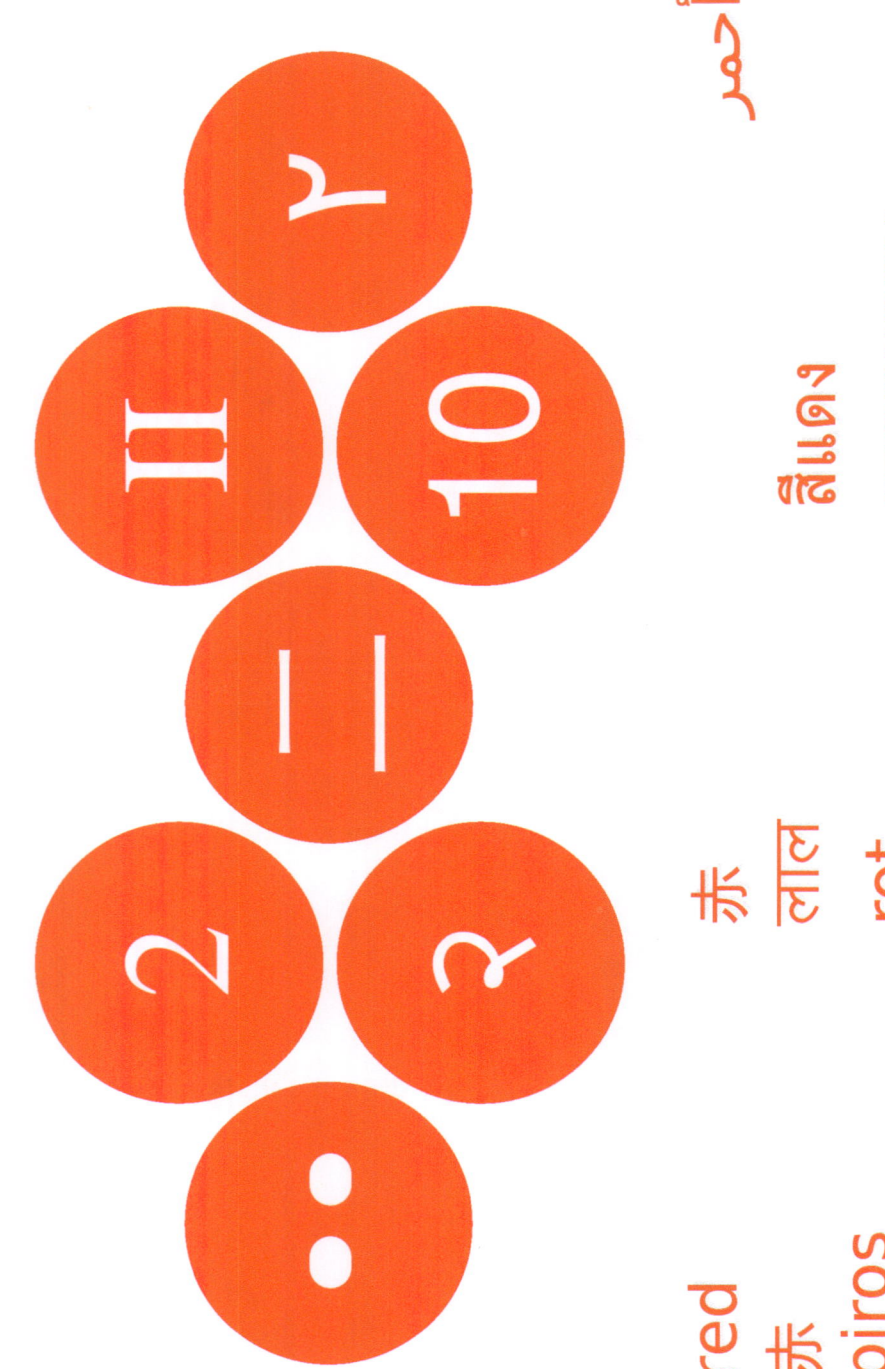

احمرَ

אדוֹם

قِرمِز

ใหแดง czerwony rood đỏ pula červená

rood

赤 रोत rosso rød vermelho nyekundu κόκκινο लाल
लाल

red
赤
piros
rouge
빨간색
ula ula
rojo
красный
অৰণ্বৰ্হ্ন

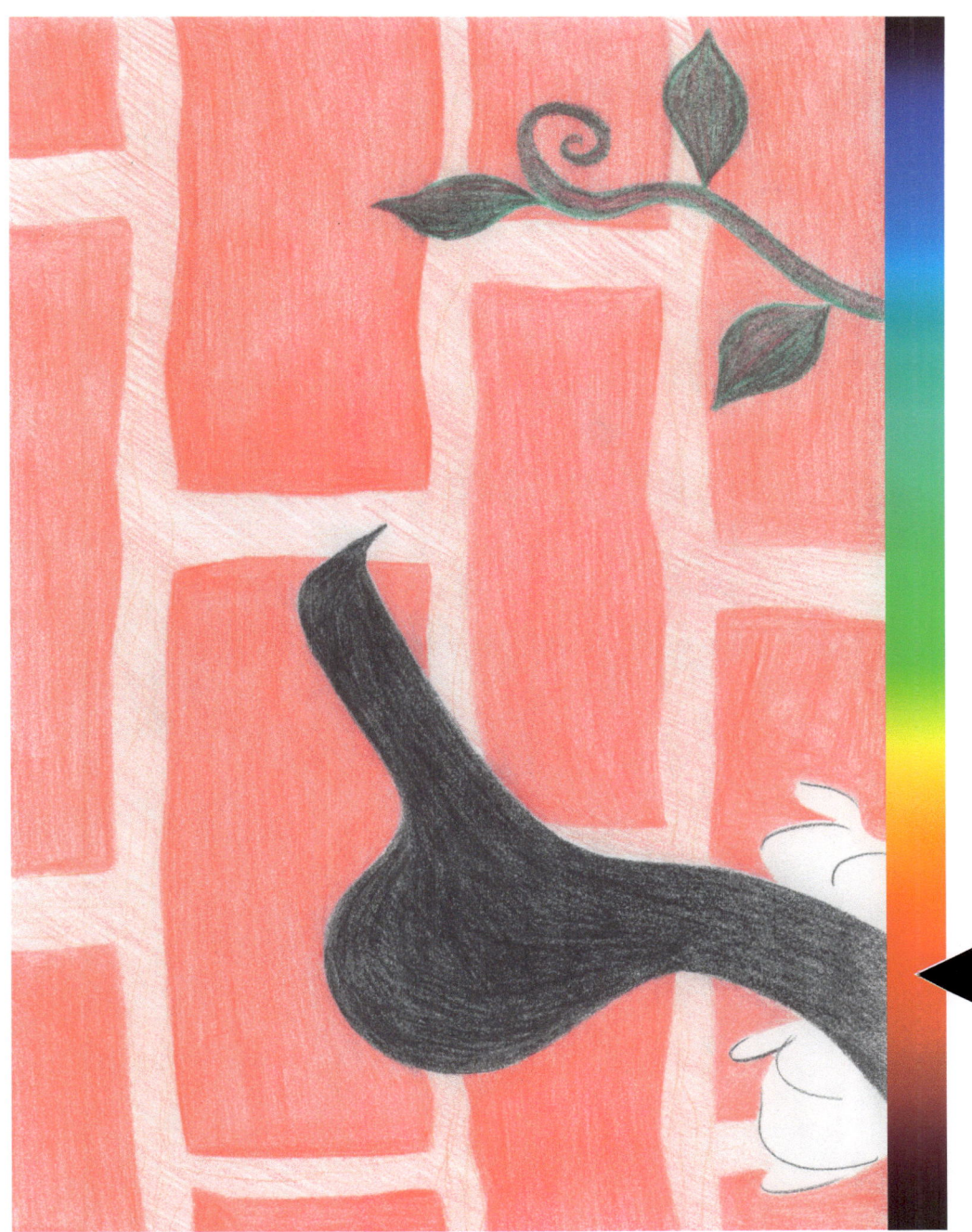

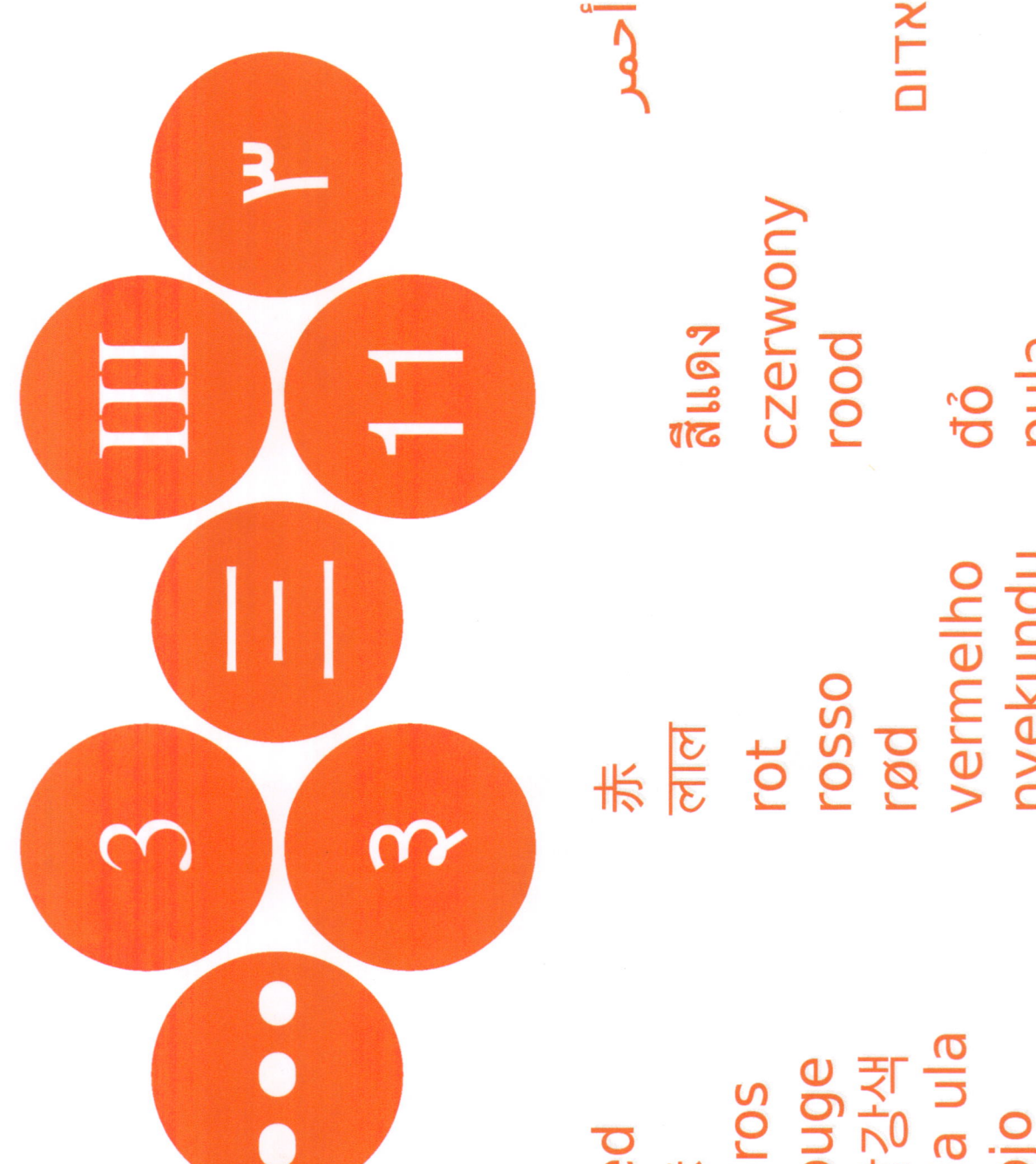

أحمر

אדום

قرمز

สีแดง
czerwony
rood

đỏ
pula
červená

赤
लाल
rot
rosso
rød
vermelho
nyekundu
κόκκινο
लाल

red
赤
piros
rouge
빨간색
ula ula
rojo
красный
ఎరుపు

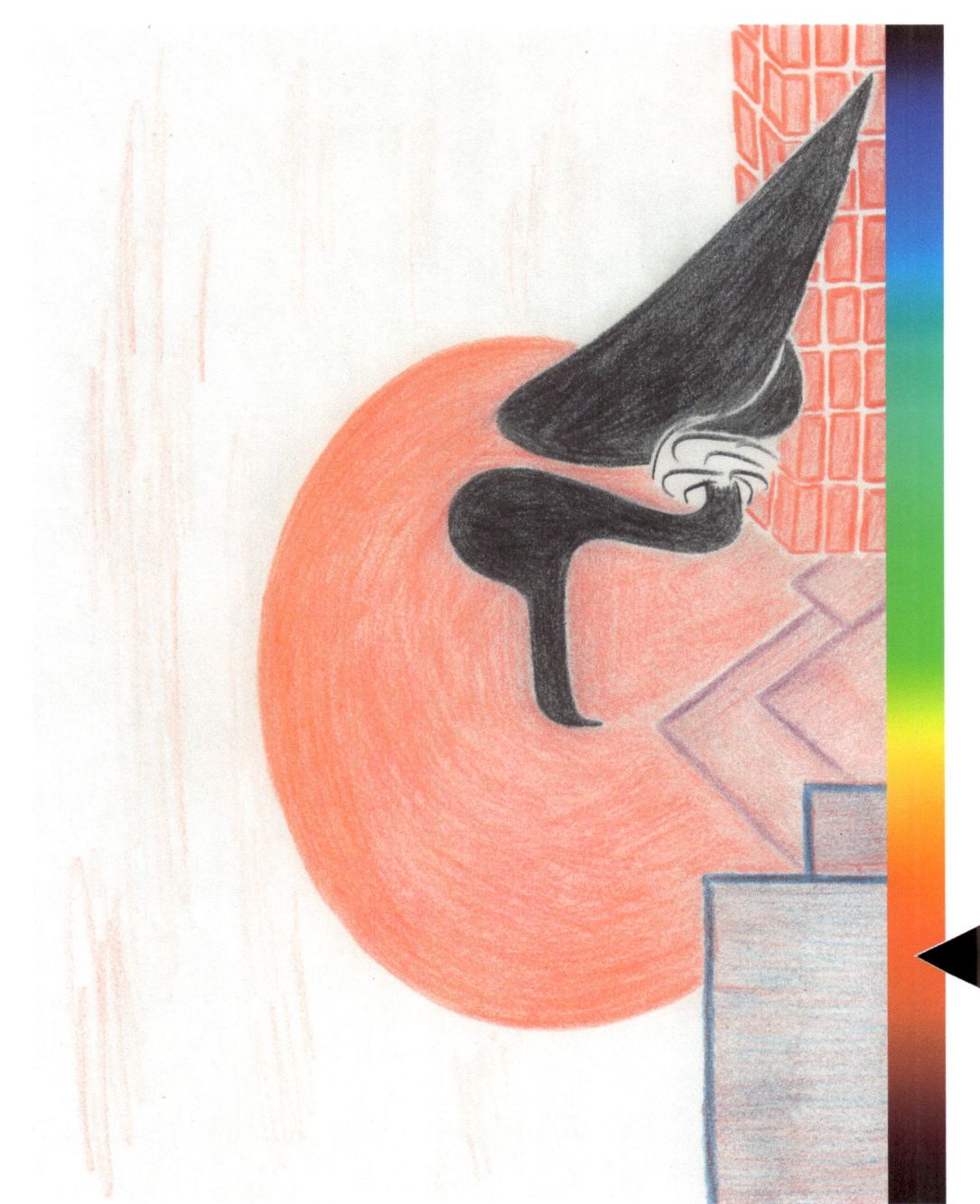

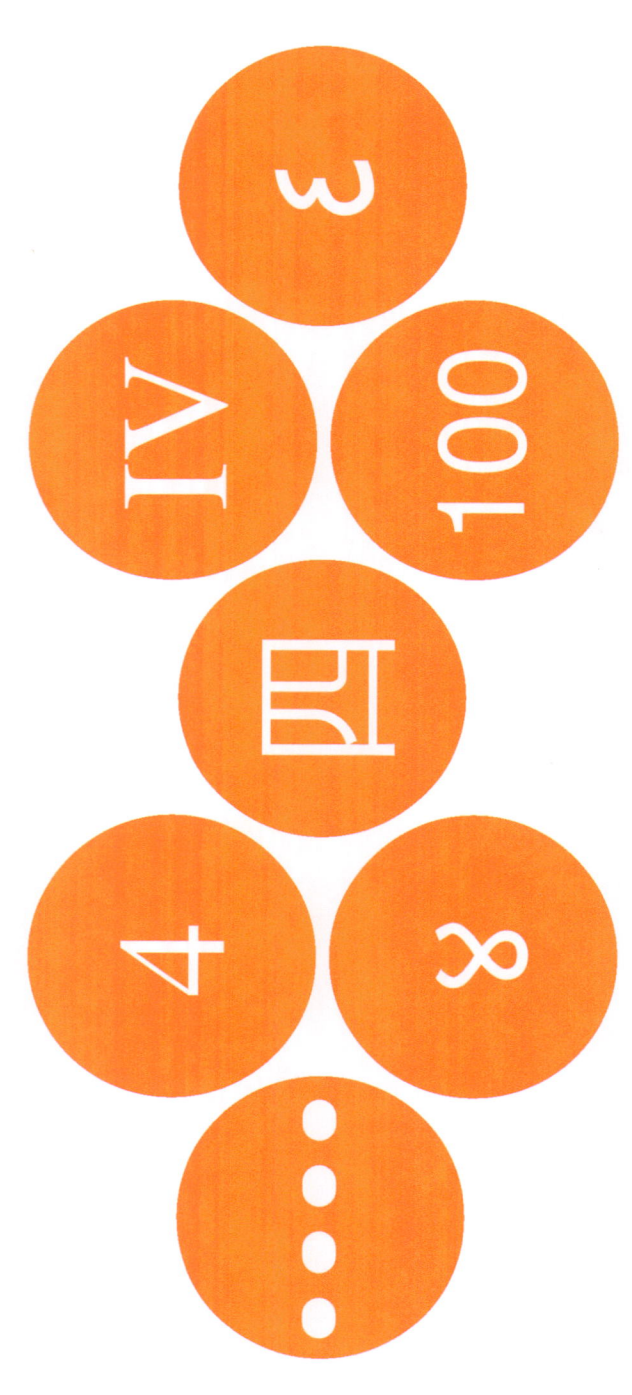

برتقالي
نارنجی

माल्टा

ম্যাট

নাৰিকল
橙色
नारंगी का

പൂസ്

orange
arancione
oransje
alaranjado
machungwa
πορτοκάλι

कलाएँ

pomarańczowy
oranje

כתום

cam
kahel
oranžová

orange
橙
narancssárga
orange
주황색
alani
naranja
оранжевый
ꩰ‌ꩢꩣ‌ꩢꩣ‌

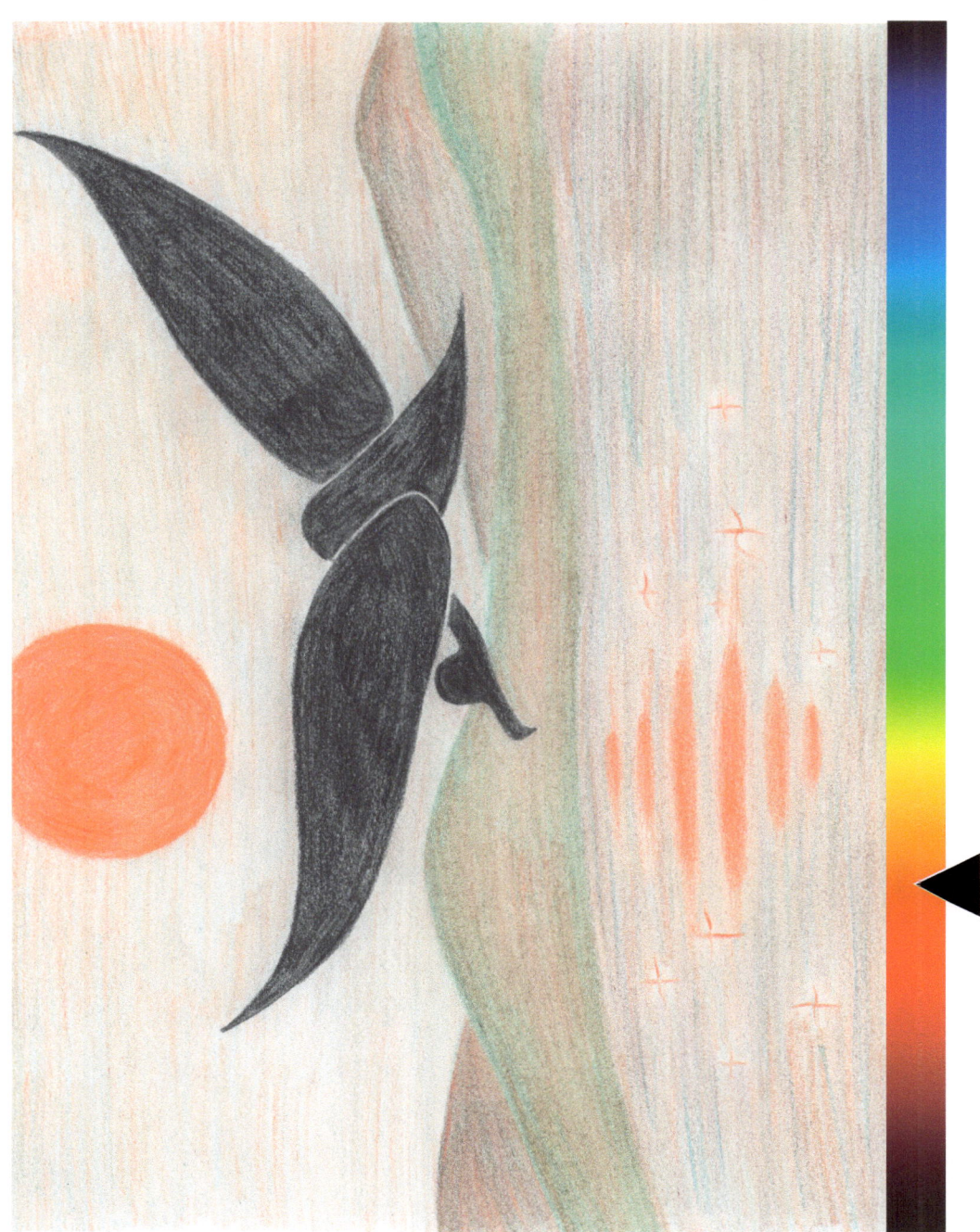

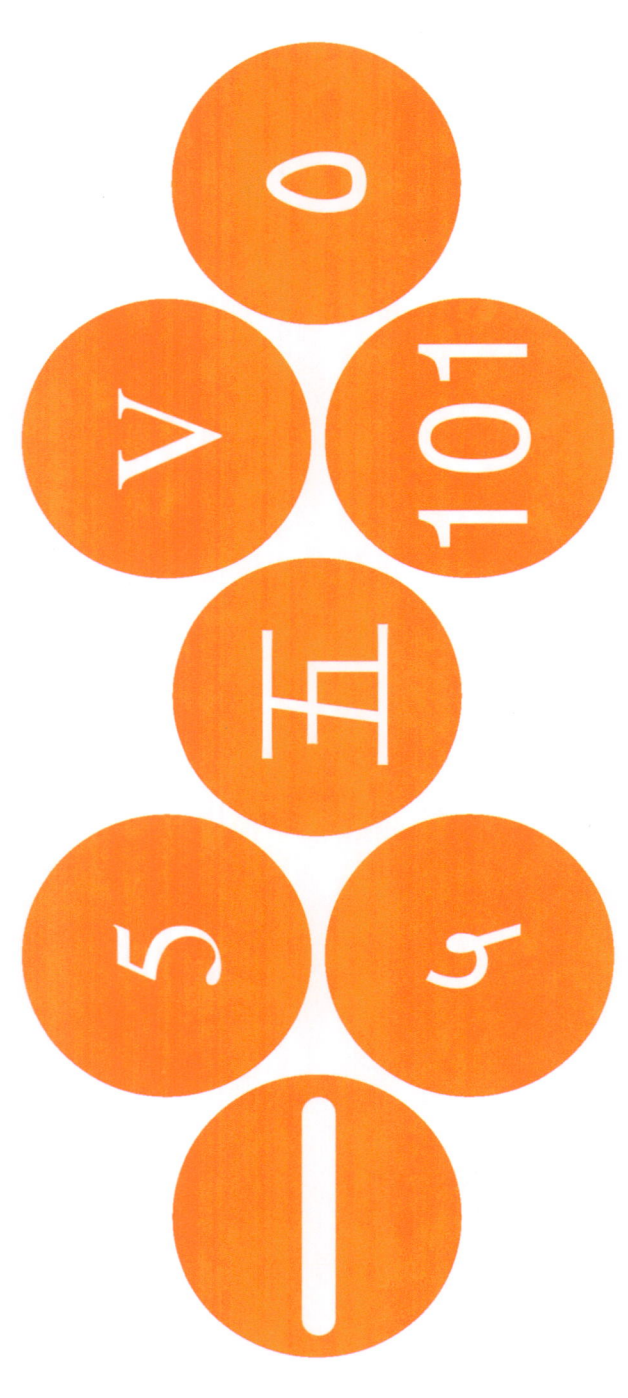

برتقالي

مۇز

پ

پ

orange
橙
narancssárga
orange
주황색
alani
naranja
оранжевый
ఓరెంజ్ రంగు

橙色
नारंगी का
orange
arancione
oransje
alaranjado
machungwa
портокάλι
କମଳା

मिथ

pomarańczowy
oranje

cam
kahel
oranžová

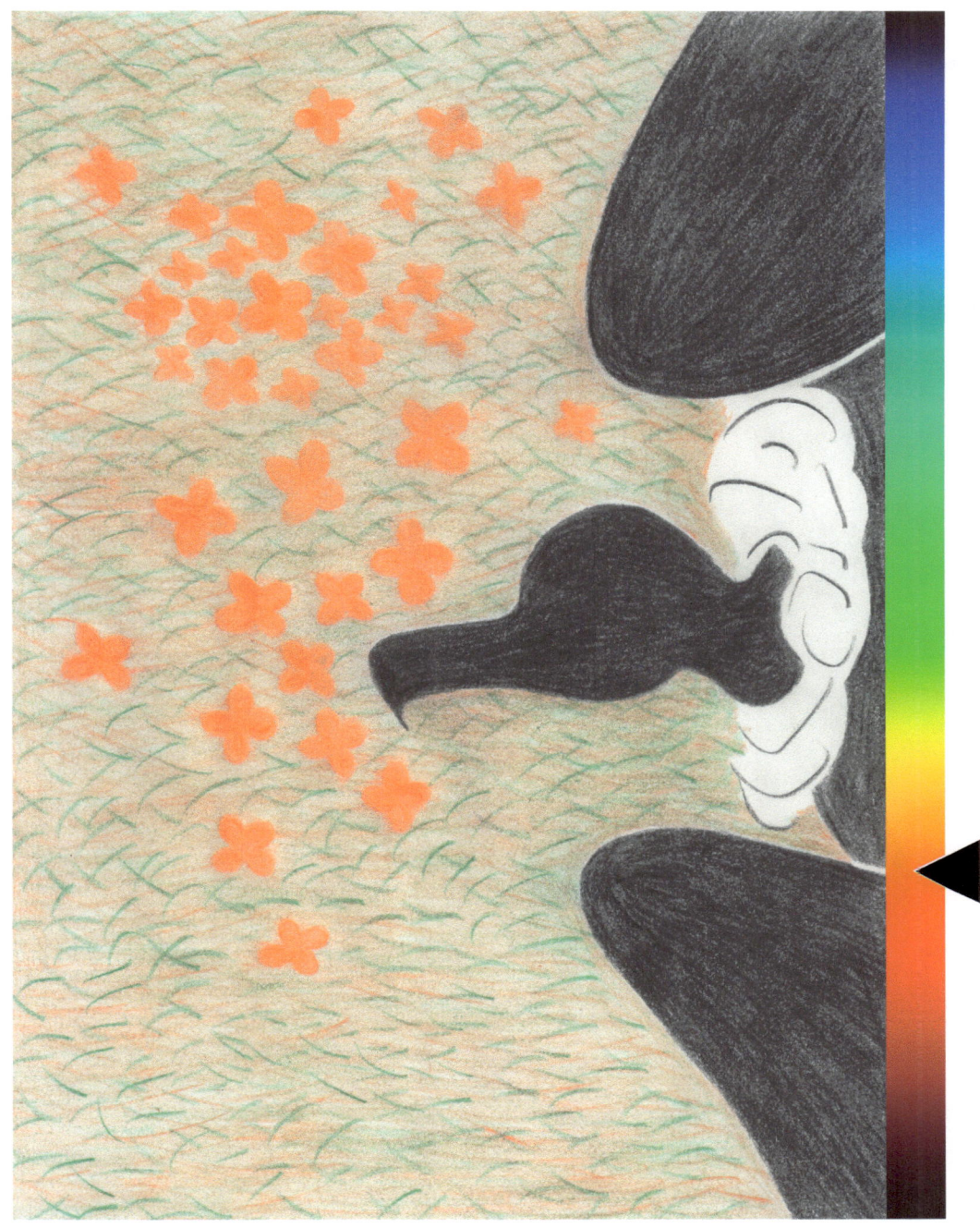

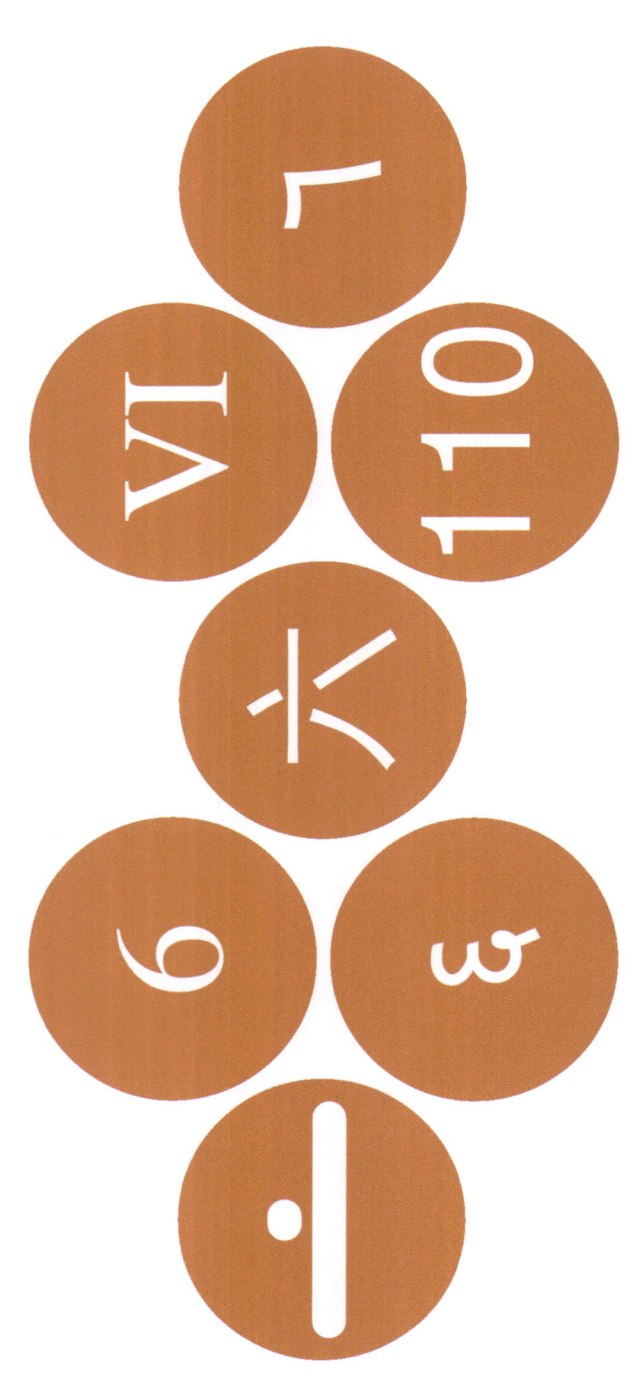

بني

DIN

قهوهای

สีน้ำตาล
brązowy
bruin

nâu
moreno
hnědá

茶色
भूरा
braun
marrone
brun
marrom
kahawia
καφέ
বাদামি

brown
褐色
barna
brun
갈색
maku'e
marrón
коричневый
ఇవారింగ్

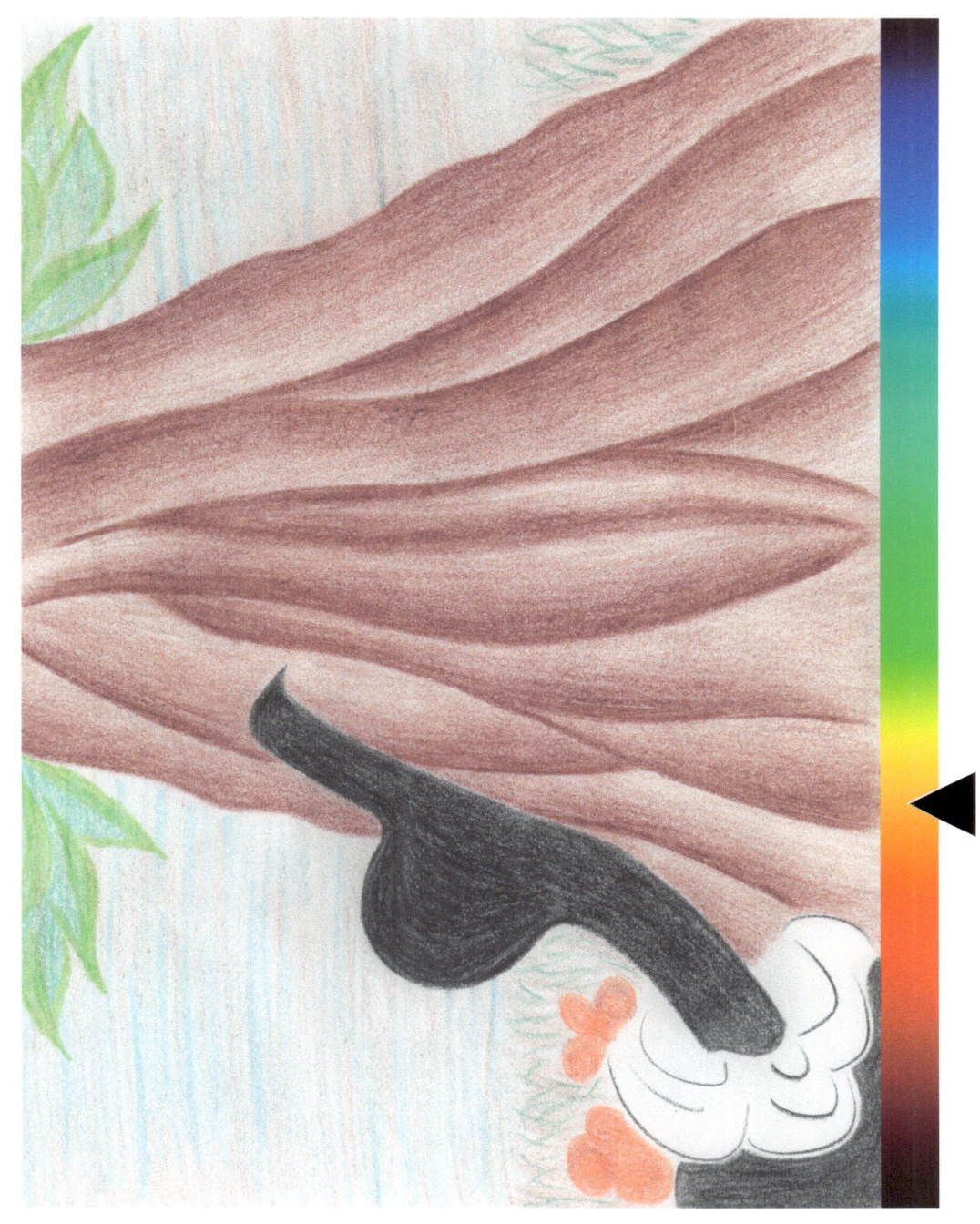

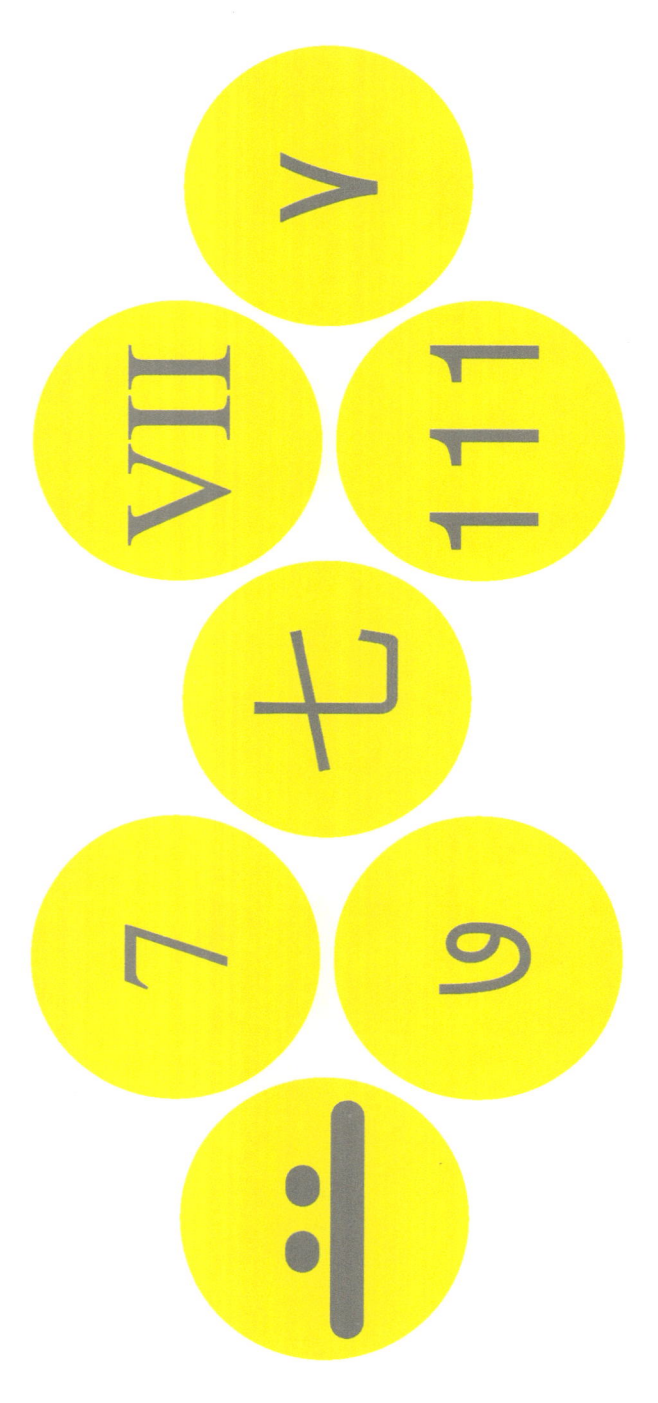

أصفر צהוב زرد

สีเหลือง żółty geel

vàng dilaw žlutá

गेल gelb giallo gul amarelo manjano κίτρινο ২৩৪

黄 पीला

yellow
黄 sárga jaune 노랑색 melemele amarillo жёлтый ಹಳದಿ

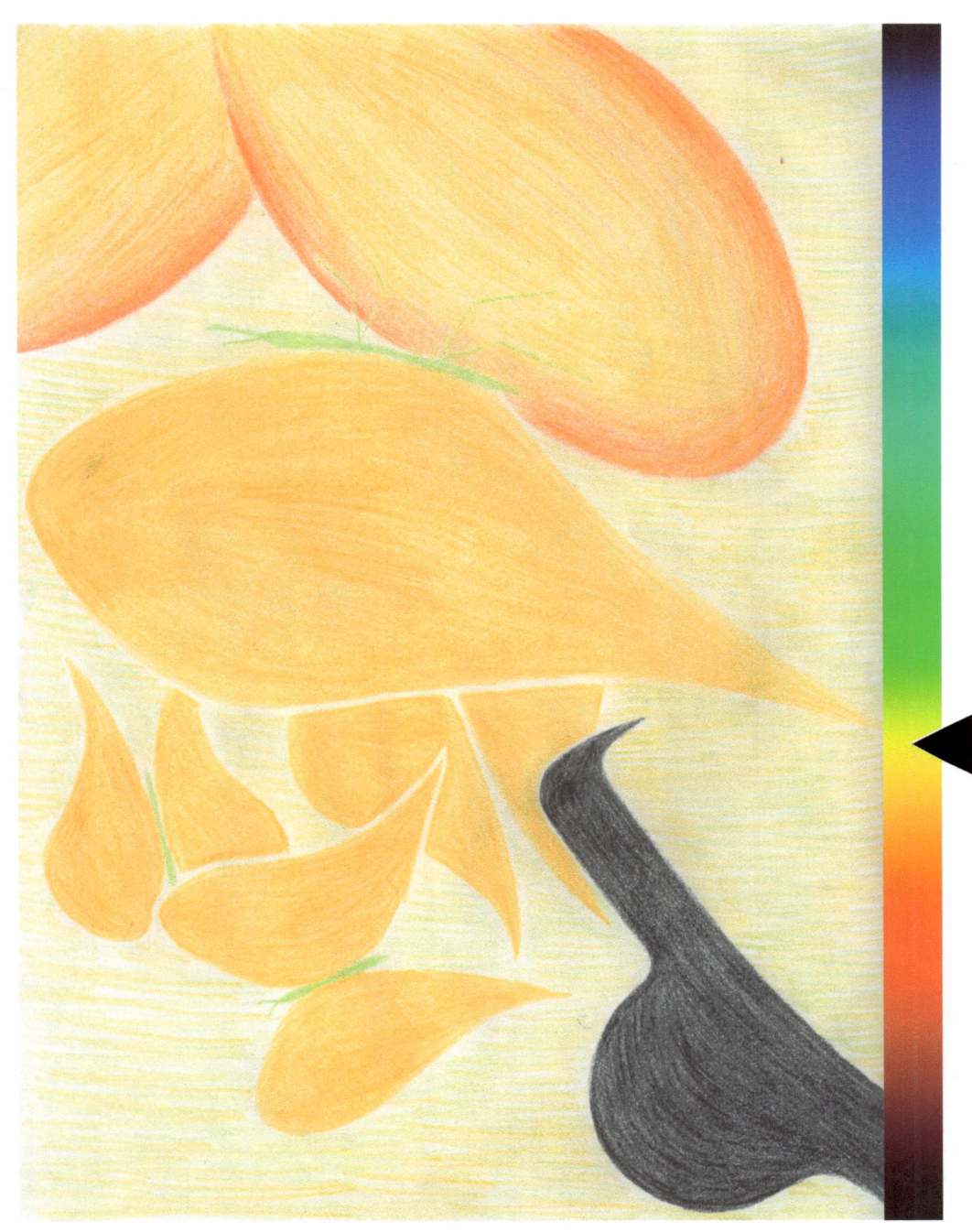

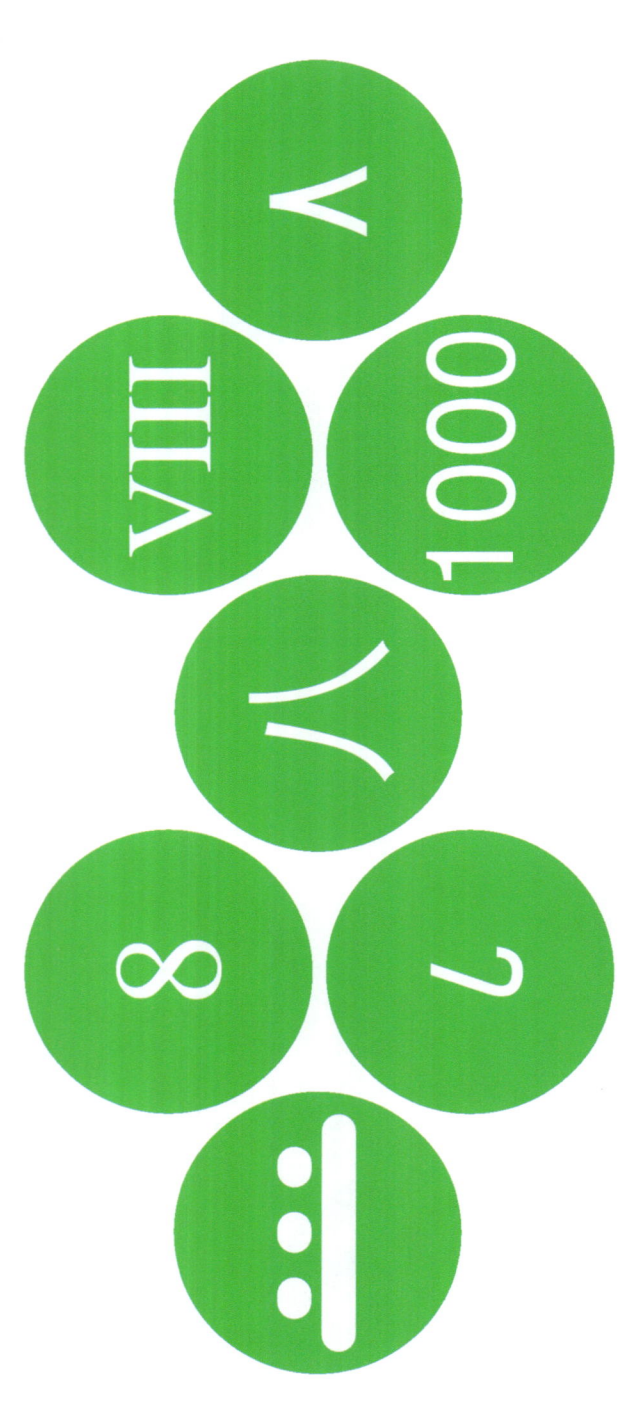

बीच्य
zielony
groene

יֶרֶק
xanh lá cây
berde
zelená

綠
हरा
grün
verde
grønn
verde
kijani
πράσινο
সবুজ

green
綠
zöld
vert
초록색
oma'oma'o
verde
зелёный
အစိမ်းရောင်

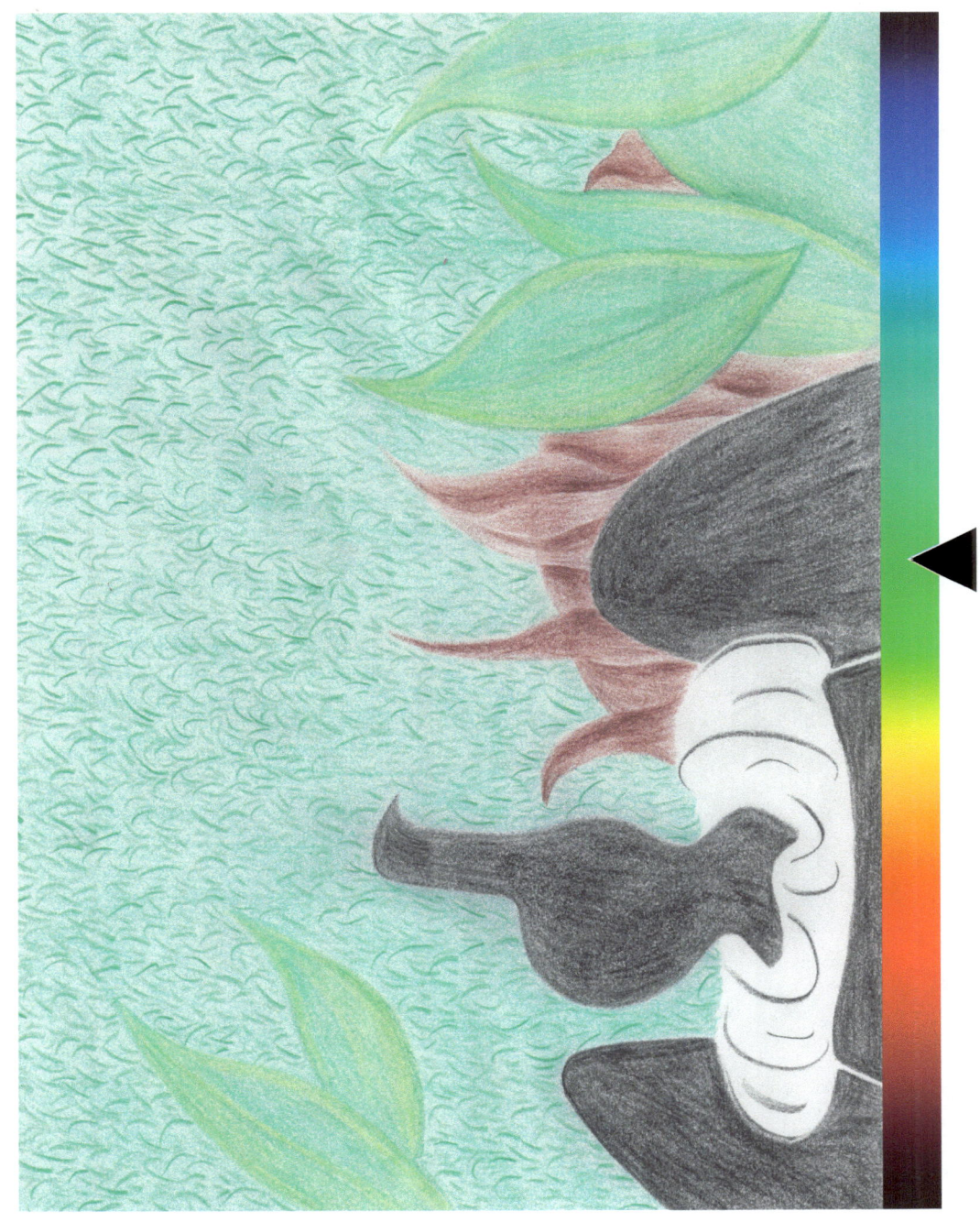

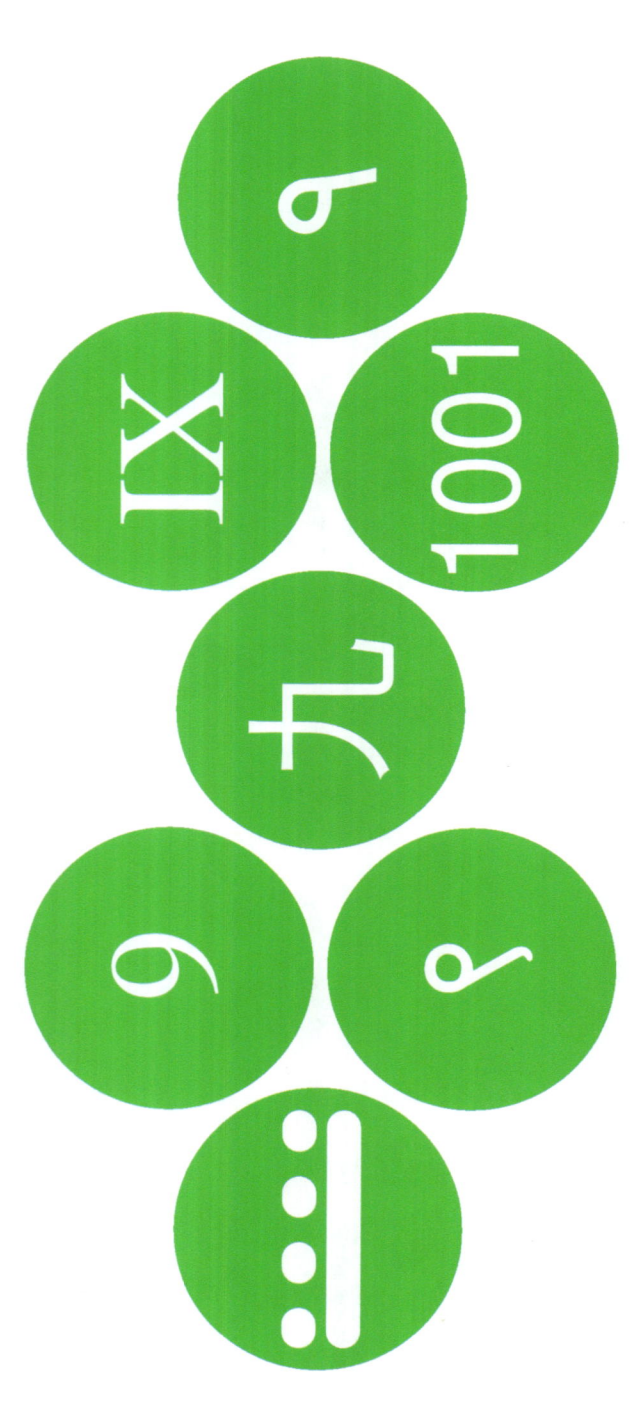

أخضر

ירוק

سبز

ลีลียว
zielony
groene

xanh lá cây
berde
zelená

grün
verde
grønn
verde
kijani
πράσινο

绿
हरा

green
绿
zöld
vert
초록색
oma'oma'o
verde
зеленый
အစိမ်းရောင်

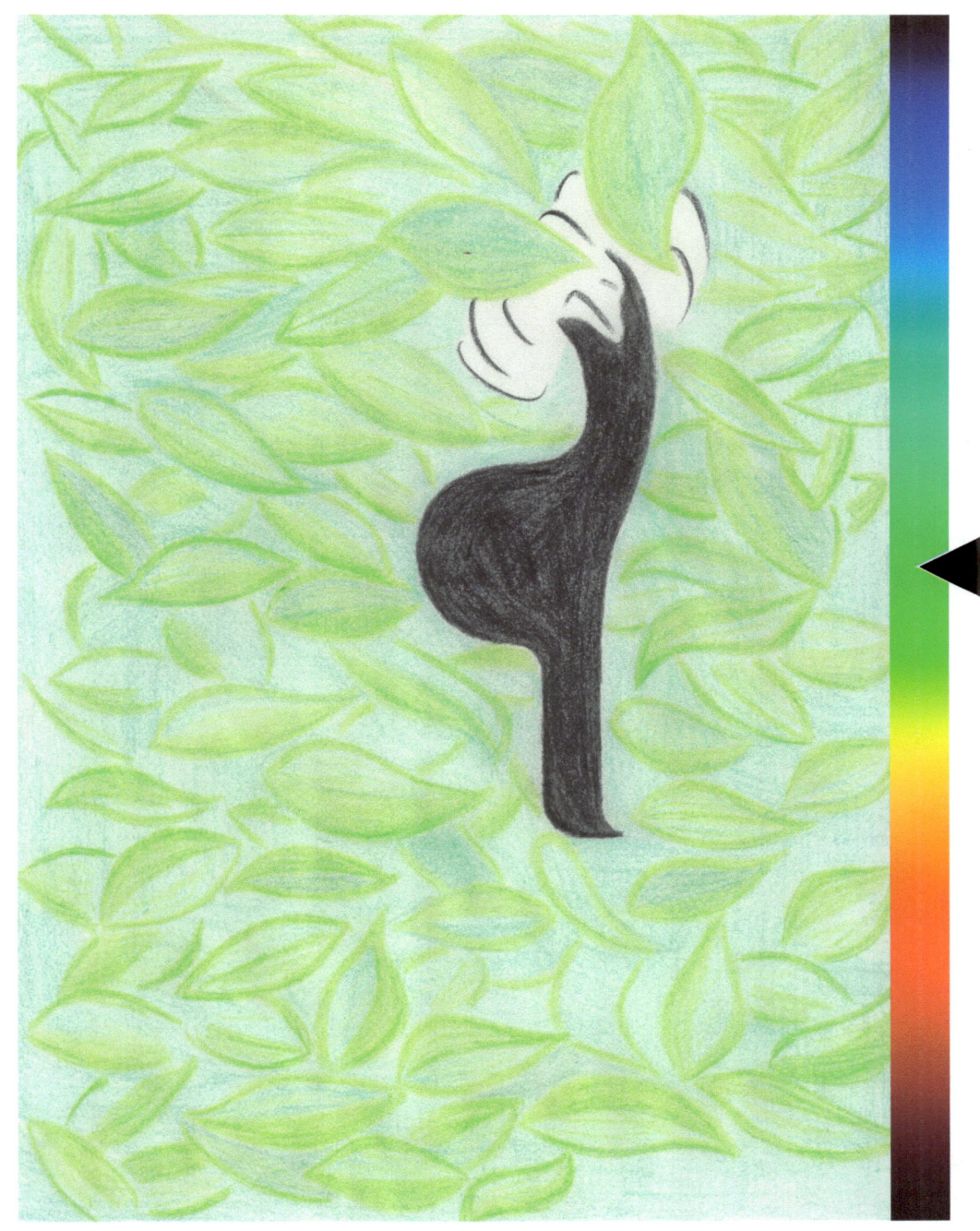

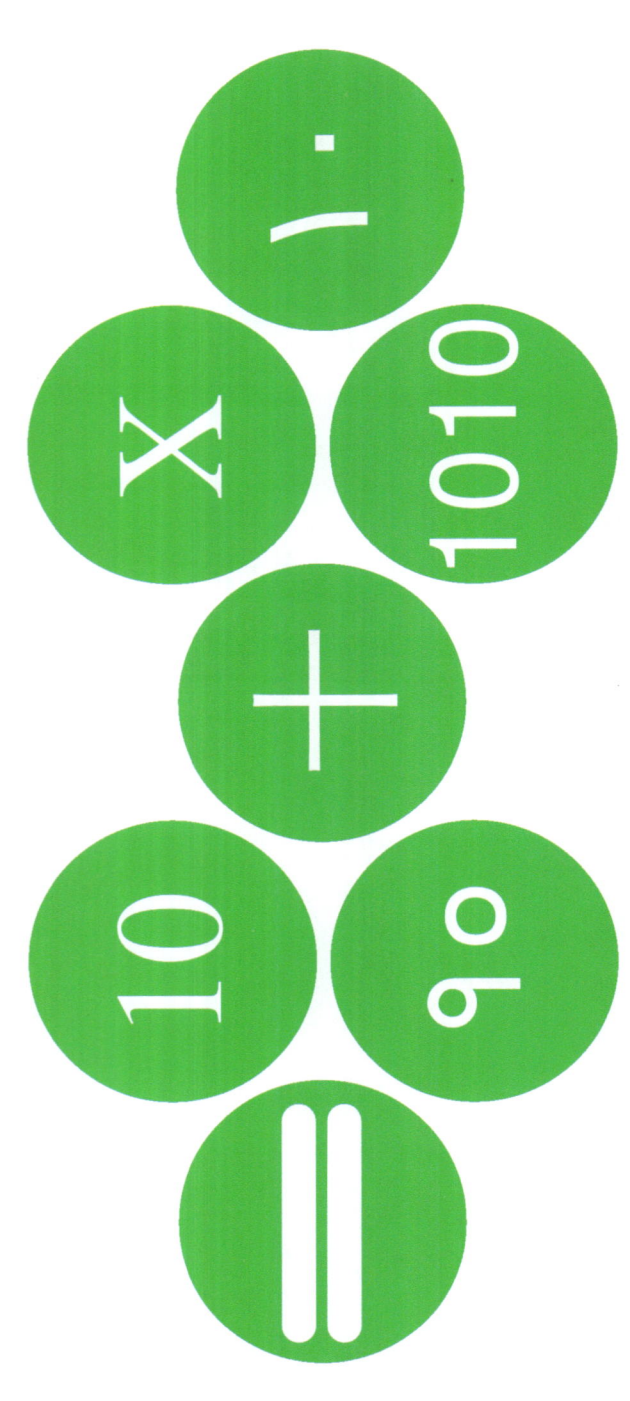

أخضر

سبز

緑 हरा grün verde grønn verde kijani πράσινο

भाषा zielony groene xanh lá cây berde zelená

ירוק

green
緑
zöld
vert
초록색
oma'oma'o
verde
зеленый

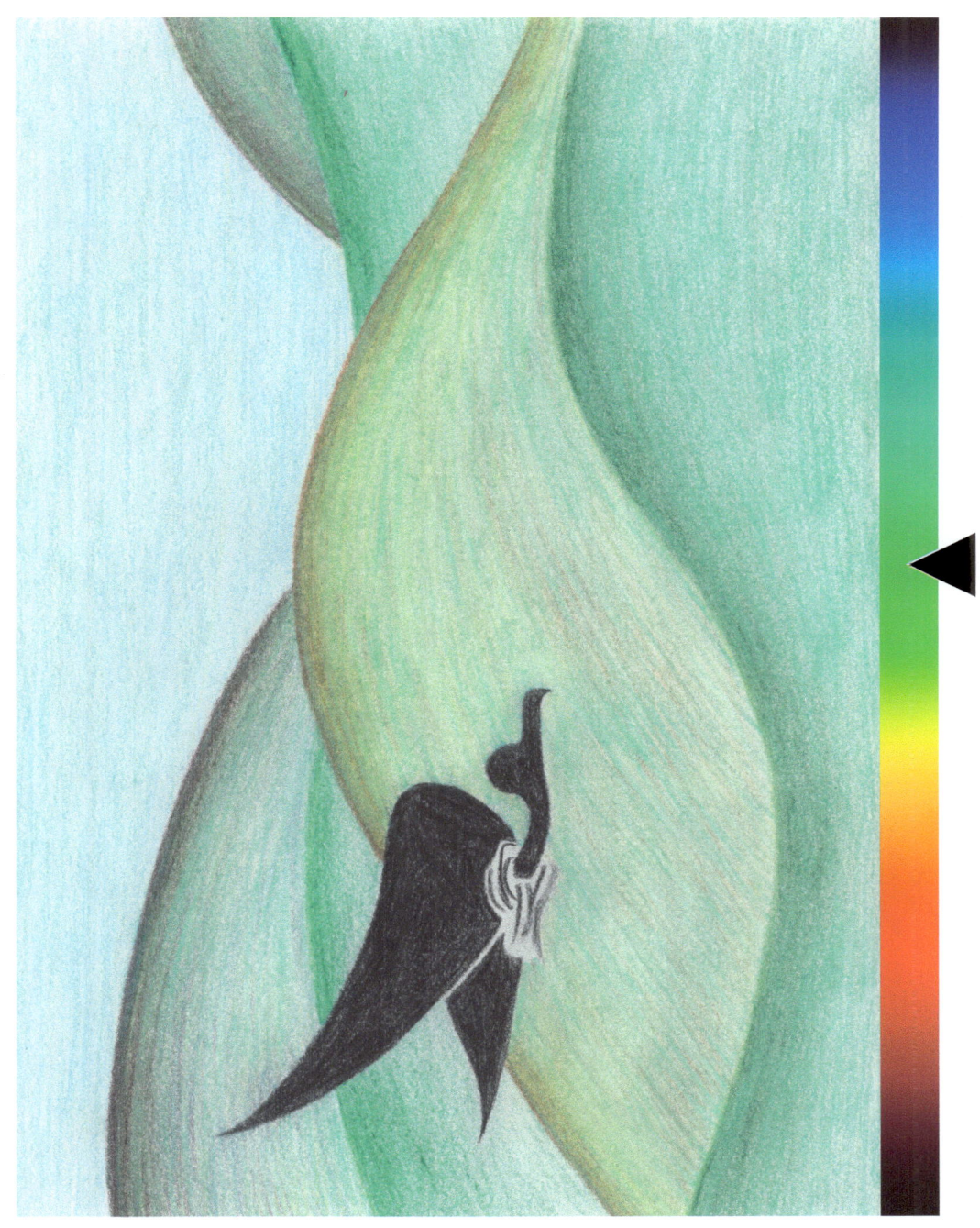

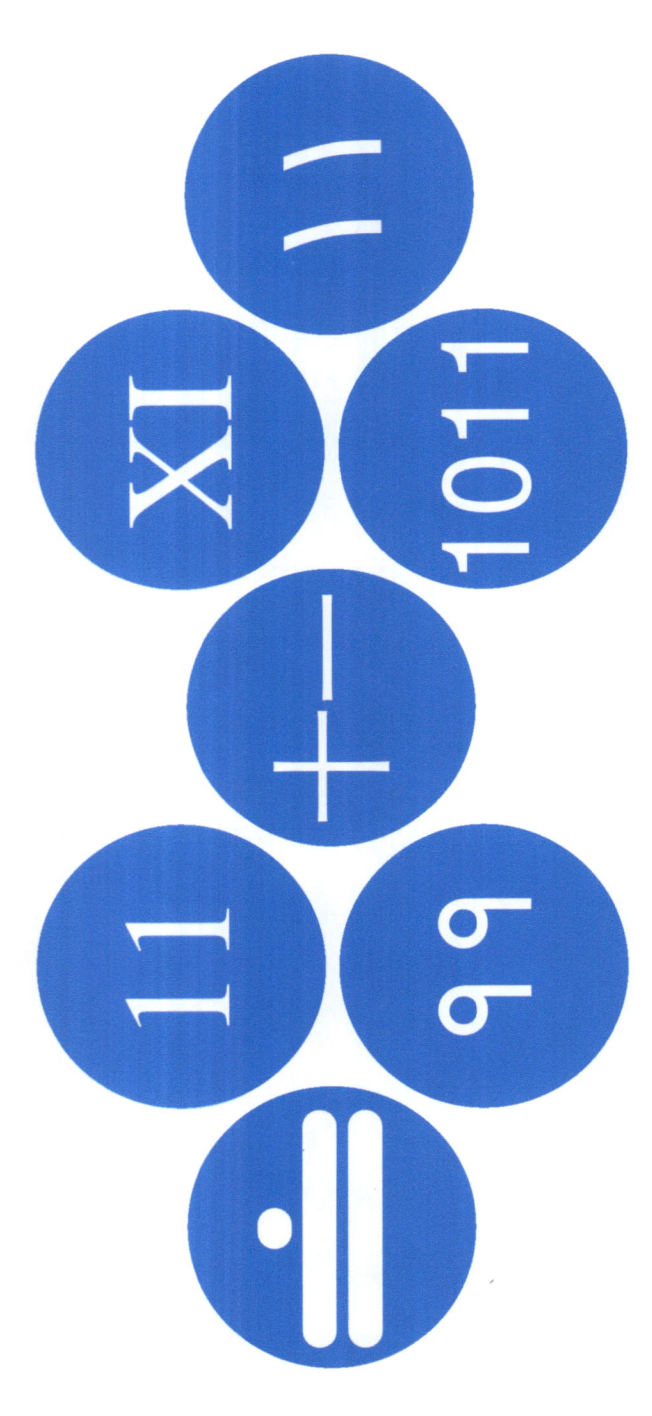

أَنَّ

أزْرَق

น้ำเงิน
niebieski
blauwe
xanh da trời
bughaw
modrá

青
नीला
blau
azzurro
blå
azul
buluu
μπλε
নীল

blue
蓝
kék
bleu
파랑색
polu
azul
синий
ఏదో

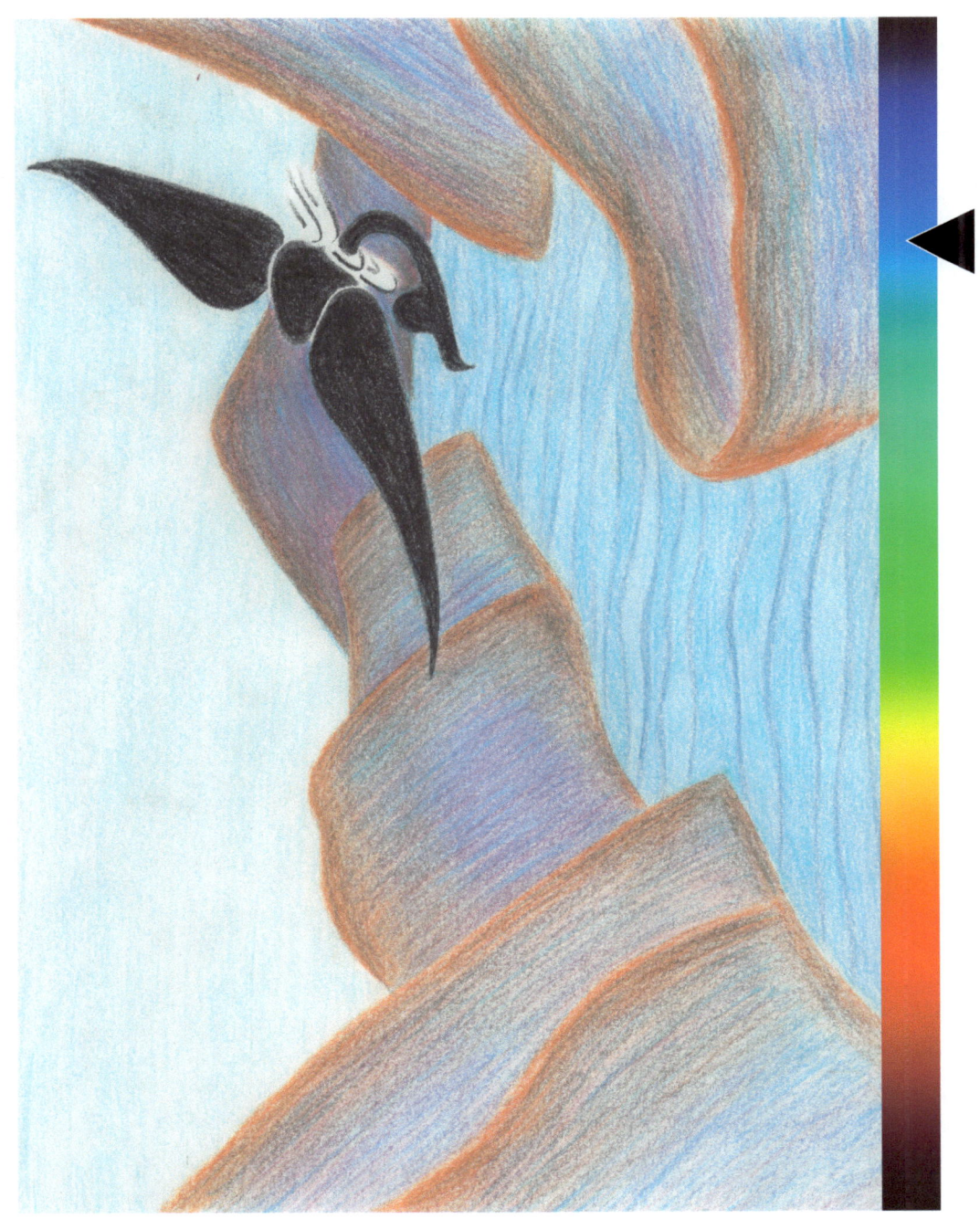

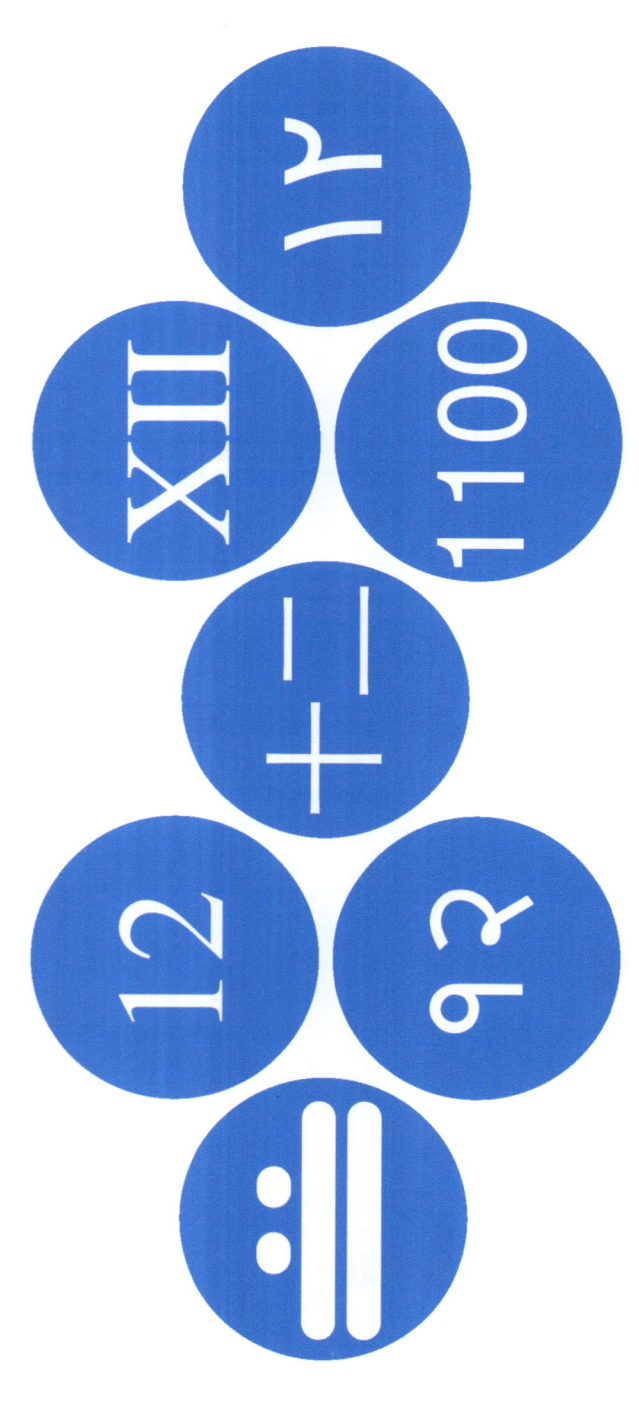

أزرق

أنت

ฟ้า

สีน้ำเงิน

niebieski

blauwe

כחל

xanh da trời

bughaw

modrá

青

नीला

blau

azzurro

blå

azul

buluu

μπλε

নিল

blue

藍

kék

bleu

파랑색

polu

azul

синий

ఇలేటంసిగ

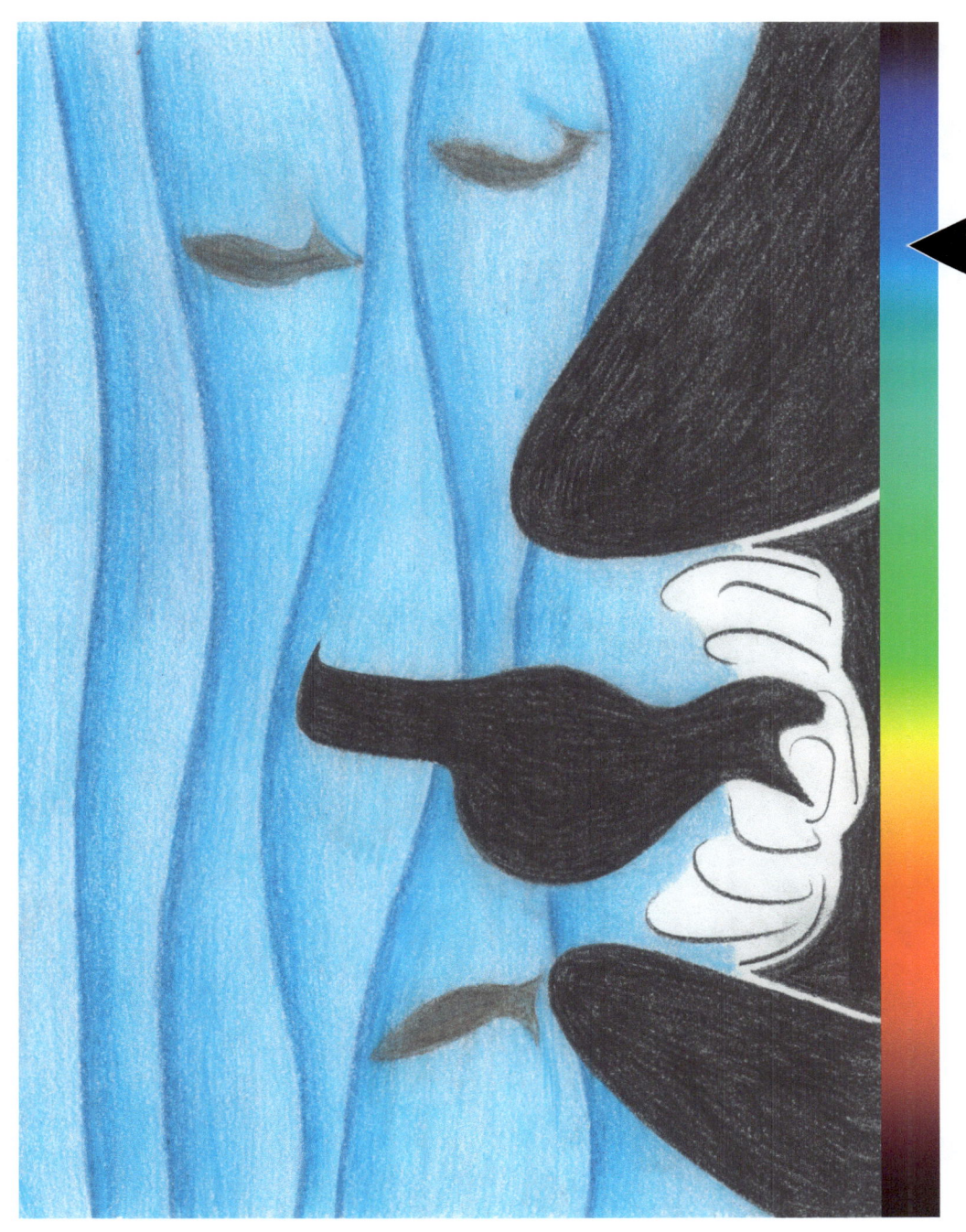

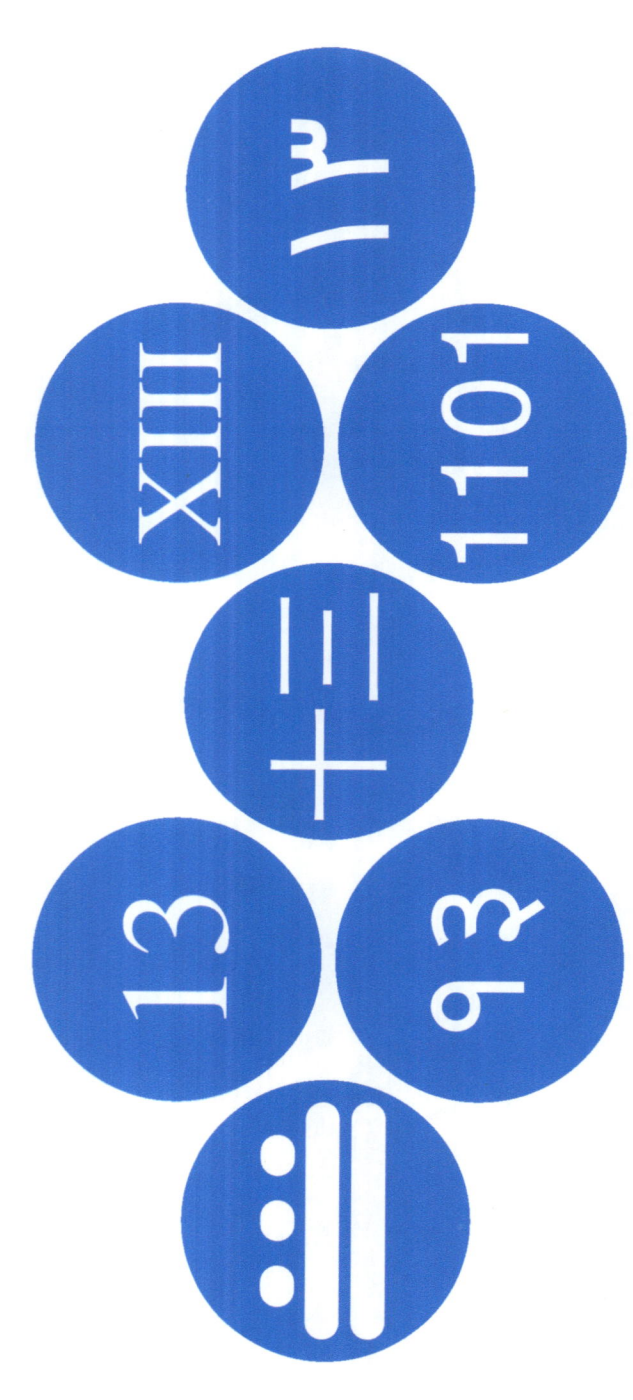

أزرق

כחול

أزل

ฟ้า/สีน้ำเงิน
niebieski
blauwe
xanh da trời
bughaw
modrá

青
नीला
blau
azzurro
blå
azul
buluu
μπλε
নীল

blue
蓝
kék
bleu
파랑색
polu
azul
синий
ಅಕಾಶನೀಲಿ

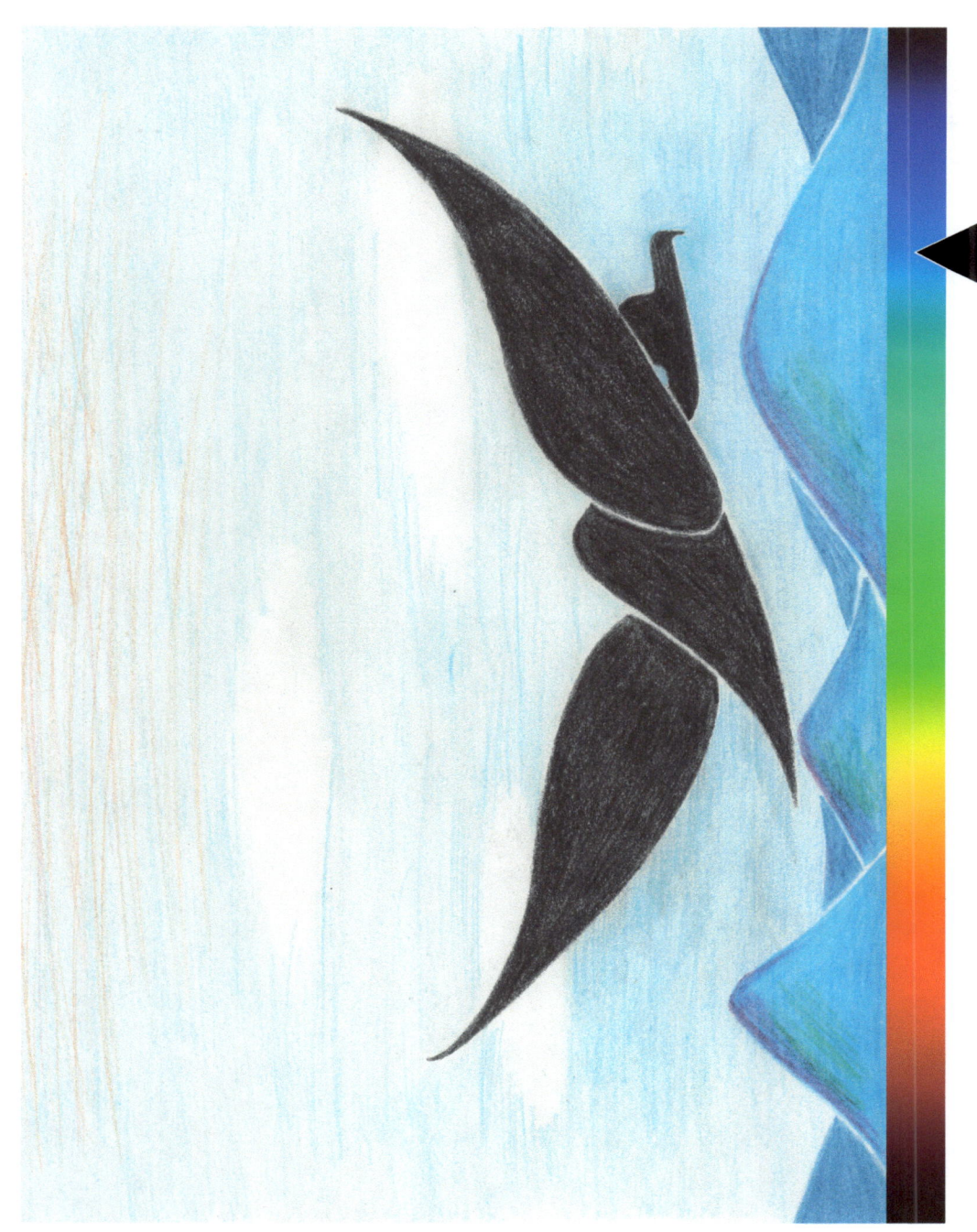

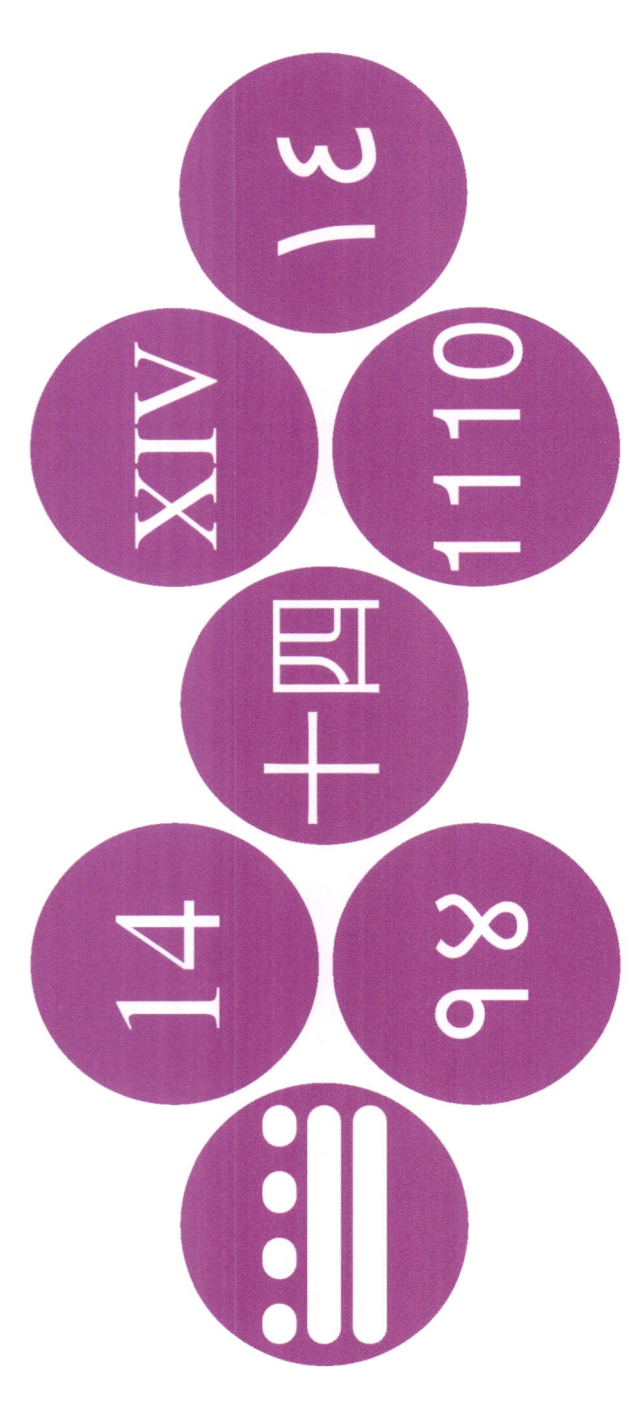

أرجواني

סגול

بنفسجي

ม่วง

purpurowy
purper

tím
lila
fialová

紫
बैंगनी

violett
viola
lilla
roxo
zambarau
μωβ
 বেগুনি

purple
紫
lila
violet
보라색
poni
purpúreo
фиолетовый
ወይነጠጅ

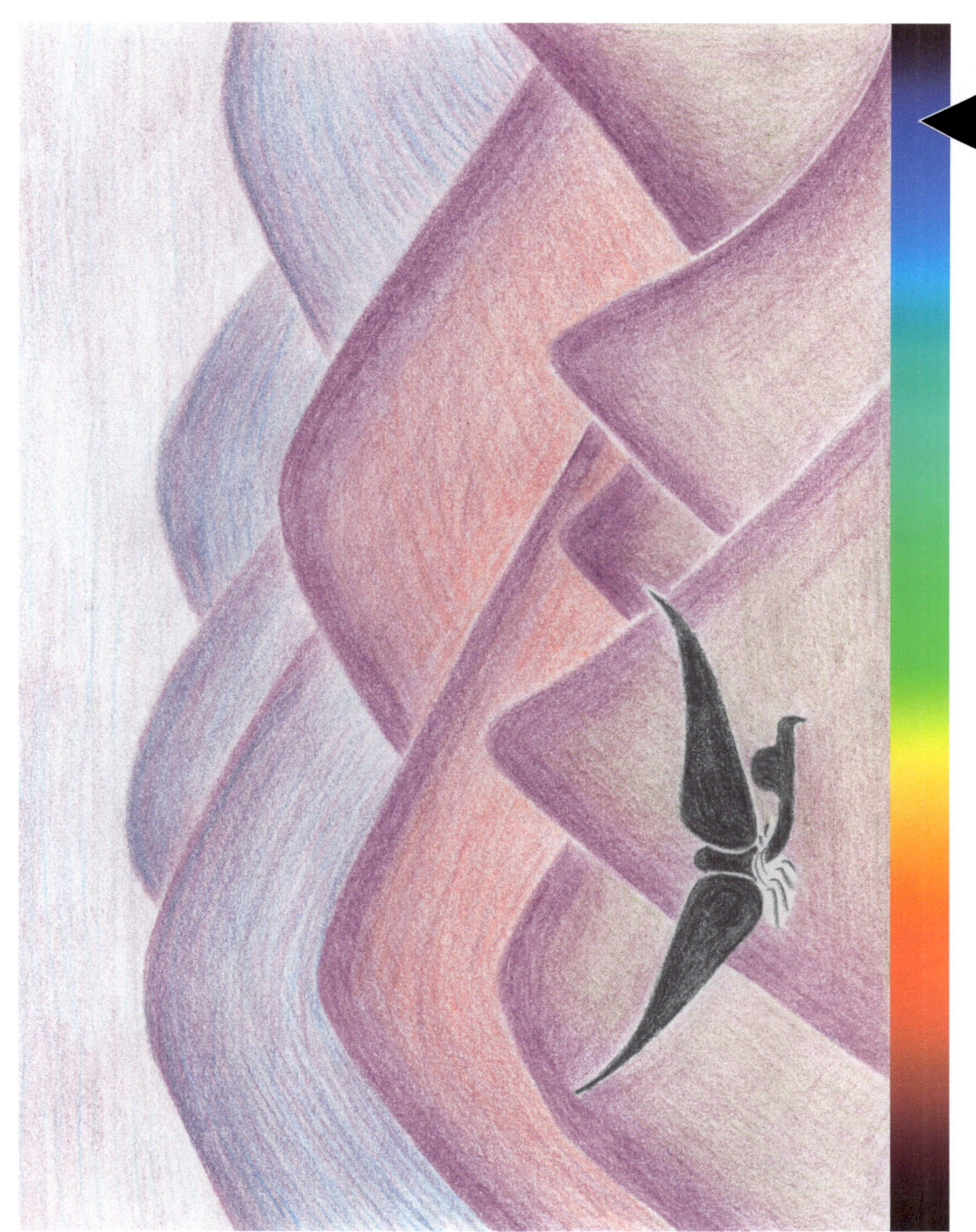

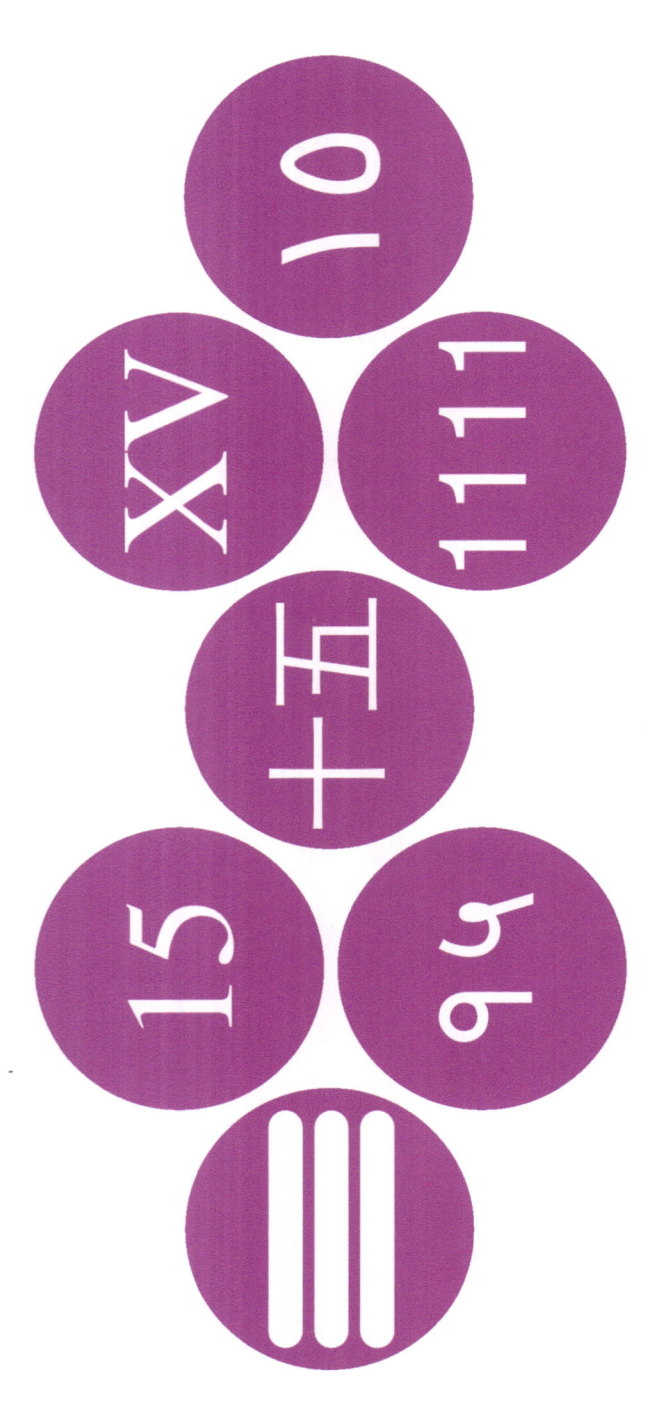

أرجواني

purpurowy
purper

סגול

ارغونی

tím
lila
fialová

紫
बैंगनी

violett
viola
lilla
roxo
zambarau
μωβ
বেগুনি

purple
lila
violet
보라색
poni
purpúreo
фиолетовый
อ่องในอ
+เจ

بنفش

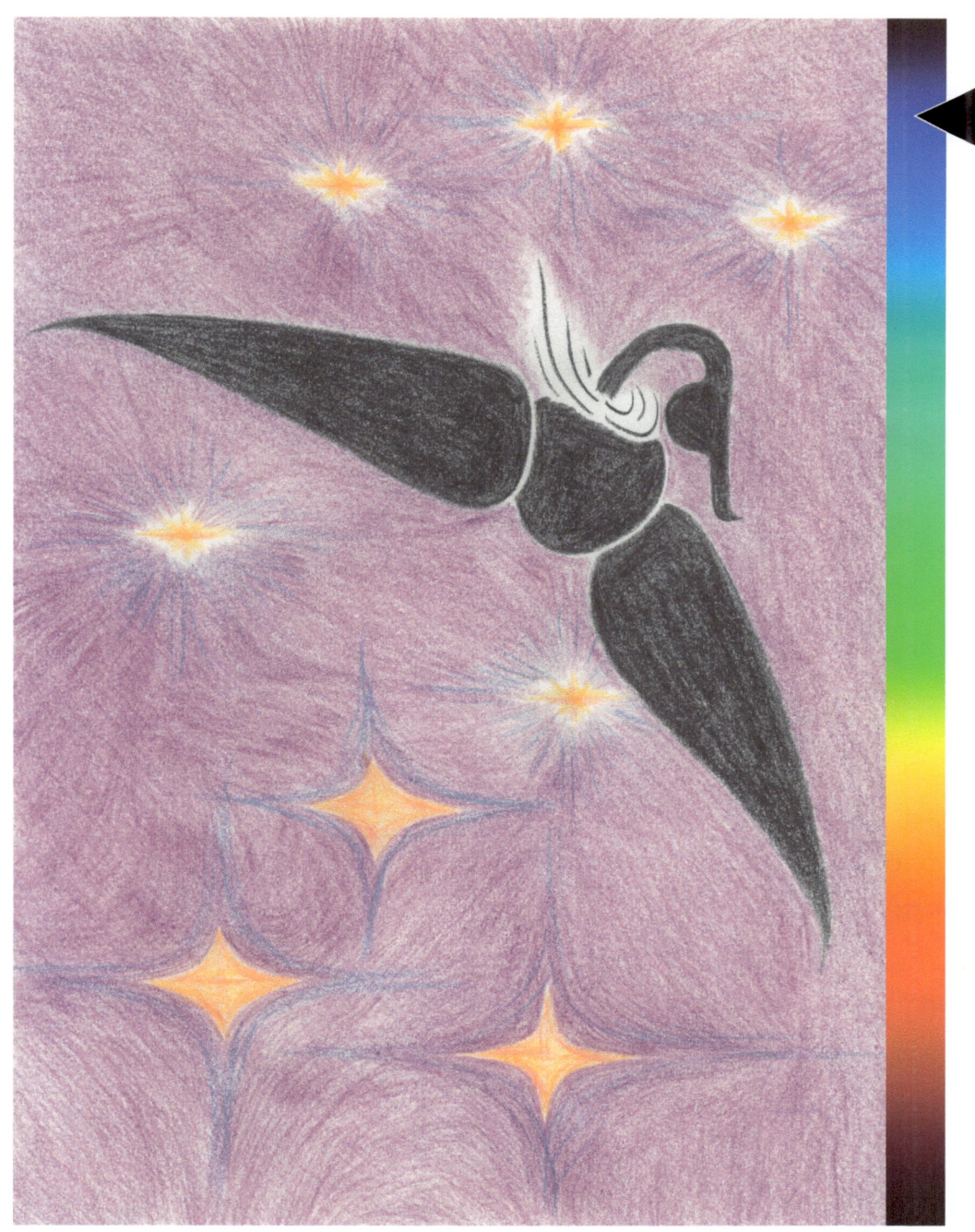

draw a face

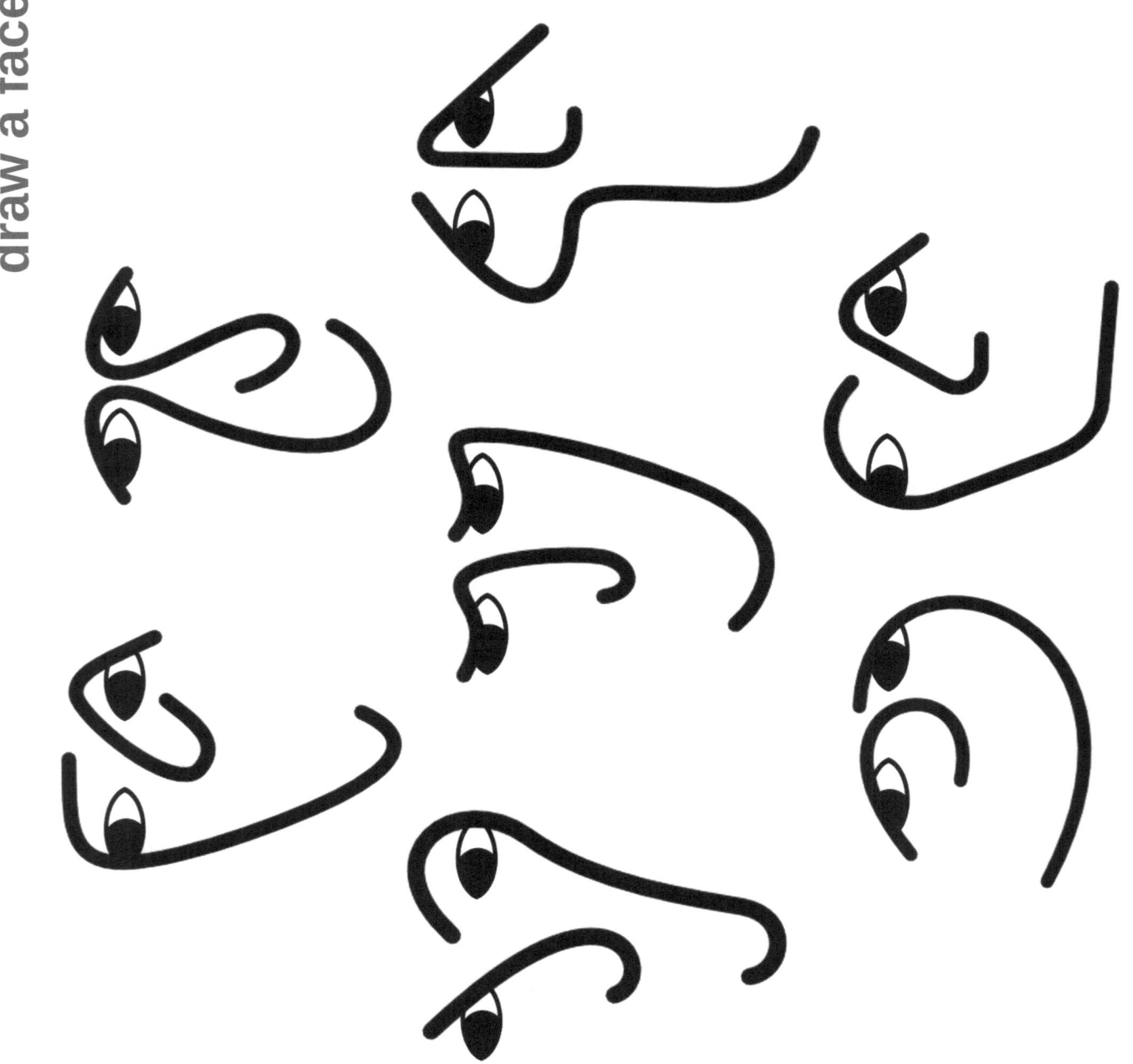

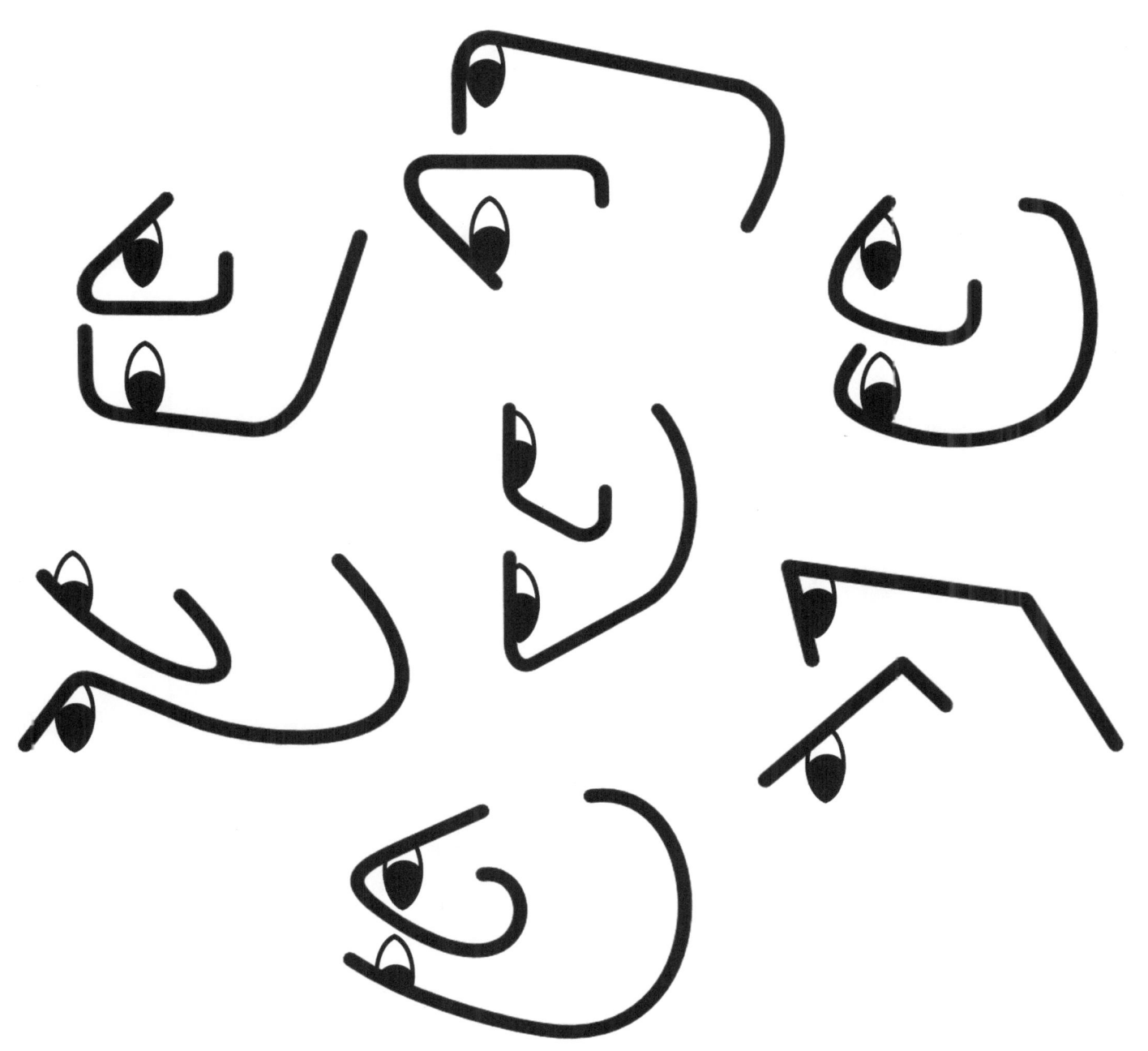

draw a person

art lessons

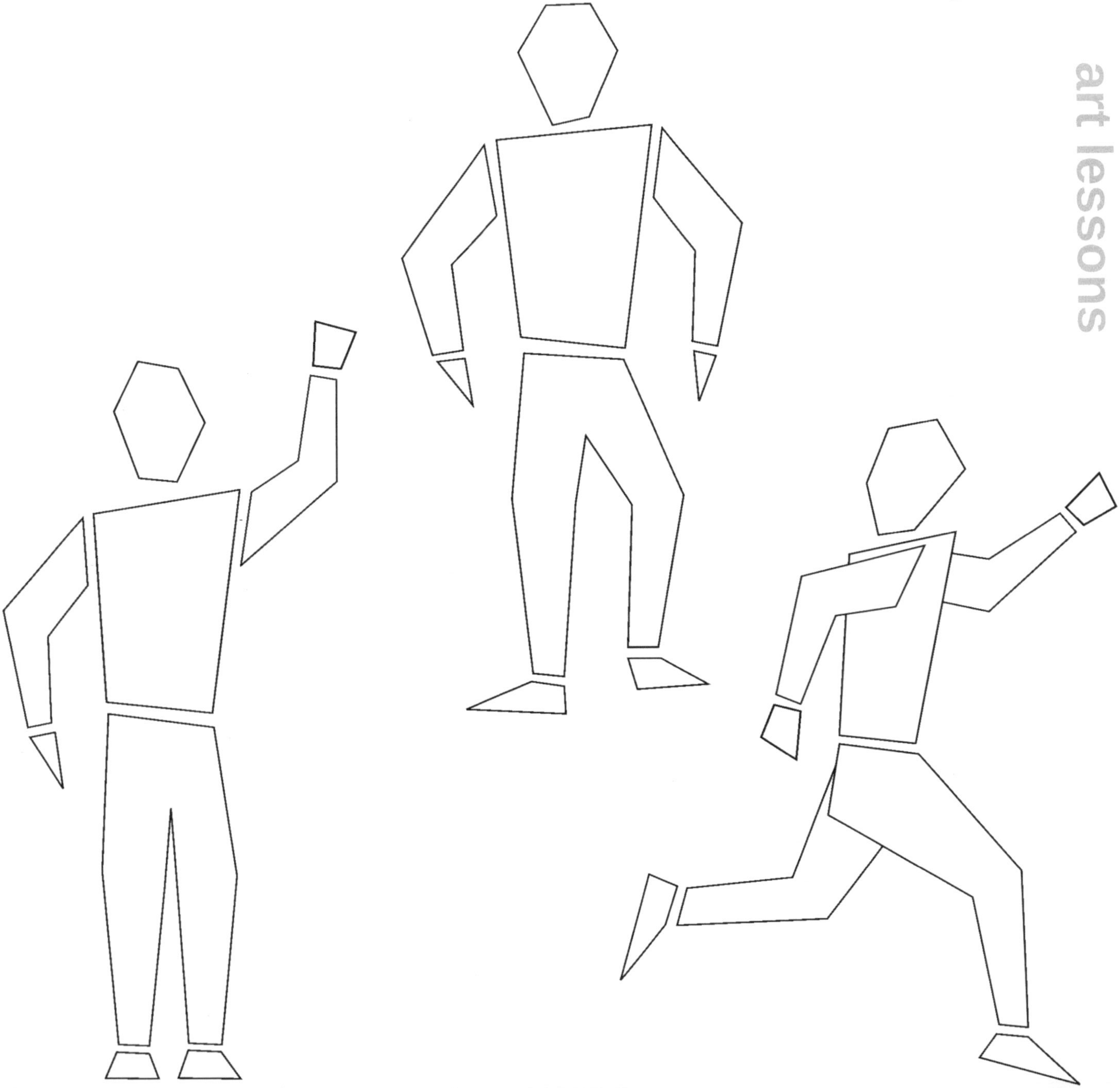

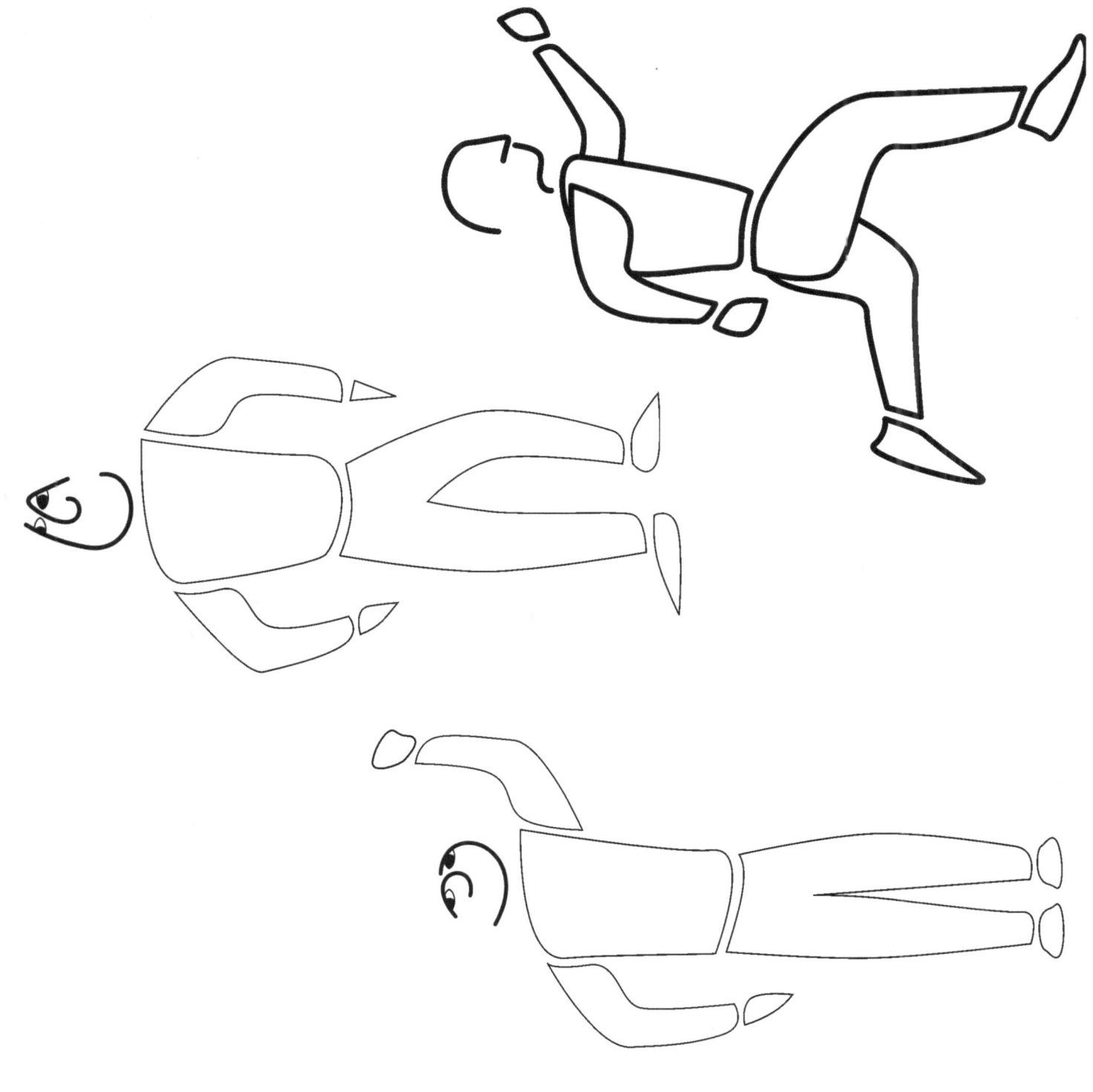

www.ingramcontent.com/pod-product-compliance
Lightning Source LLC
Chambersburg PA
CBHW050403180526
45159CB00005B/2132